THE ROLE OF THE CRITIC

Nicholas Dromgoole

The Role of the Critic

OBERON BOOKS
LONDON

For James Hogan and Charles Glanville,
whose friendship and good company have
been among my life's major pleasures.

First published in 2010 by Oberon Books Ltd

521 Caledonian Road, London N7 9RH

Tel: 020 7607 3637 / Fax: 020 7607 3629

e-mail: info@oberonbooks.com

www.oberonbooks.com

A catalogue record for this book is available from the
British Library.

ISBN: 978-1-84002-973-4

Printed in Great Britain by CPI Antony Rowe, Chippenham

Contents

The herded wolves, bold only to pursue;
The obscene ravens, clamorous o'er the dead;
The vultures , to the conqueror's banner true,
Who feed where Desolation first has fed,
And whose wings rain contagion….

(*Shelley in* 'Adonais' *on the critics*)

W HEN I FIRST met the 'significant other' who was to become my wife, I was already an established dance critic on the 'Sunday Telegraph', and she was already a leading ballerina of the Royal Ballet at Covent Garden. As can be imagined this meant there was already a certain tension, a certain 'frisson' between us. It had actually been reported in the news that an American ballerina in New York had emptied a bowl of punch over the head of an American critic, Clive Barnes, when they first met at a party. Here were we, meeting for the first time at a party. I looked round anxiously to make sure no bowl of punch was to hand. Fortunately for me she was more interested in a verbal assault. "Are you a dancer?", she asked, "Have you any idea what it feels like to go out alone on that stage watched by over two thousand people, and try to keep their attention? If not, what right have you to pass judgement on a performance? How can you possibly dare to suggest you know what you are talking about?" Although remarkably pretty, in the flesh she was smaller than I had expected, but she certainly made up for this by the combative nature of her assault. I was quite unready for such a spirited attack.

Yet I was after all a critic. Words were my stock in trade. I had my answer ready. "No", I said, "I am not a dancer. I am a writer. I do not dance, I write. And I do not write for dancers, choreographers, dance teachers or ballet directors. As, I hope, an informed member of the audience, I write for other members of the audience. I write for my equals, other members of your audience, just as I might share my views with them if we left a performance together. It is surely human nature to want to share views, to discuss and analyse, to ask why some things are successful and others fail, to compare one thing with another? And since you ask," I said, "I do dance. Perhaps you will let me show you?" And I led her on to the dance floor, where one thing led to another.

All the same, I was very much aware at the time that my answer was inadequate. Art criticism is an exacting and honourable profession. It has a long history. It is itself a branch of literature and some very grand writers indeed have been critics of the fine arts. They deserved a better defence.

First and foremost an art critic must presumably have a fairly straightforward idea of what is meant by the very word 'art', and what art is 'for'. A would–be critic must also have knowledge of the history of aesthetics and of art criticism. Alongside that must go detailed knowledge of the history and achievements of the chosen art form and also a good idea of how that art form chimes in with developments in the other fine arts of its day. Even more importantly, the critic must approach a new work of art with an open mind, trying hard to avoid precon-ceived ideas about what the artist should be doing. There is also the crucial question of humility. The critic should be humble. Critics are dealing with the work of professionals who have in most cases devoted their lives to what they create. They deserve respect. A critic may not always feel that an artist has succeeded, but he is not handing down judgements from some lofty throne. Any critic who uses a perceived failure as an opportu-nity to have an ego trip all over the page, is behaving dishonourably.

Anybody with any knowledge of art history must also be aware that all too often there have been periods when critics have done positive harm to the development of an art form, have been too dismissive of important creations, and sometimes positively obstructive. It is almost inevitable that some artists should be out of touch with later developments, or fail to appreciate the work of much younger contemporaries. We can understand why Rossini should have said of the 'Symphonie Fantasque' by Berlioz, "How fortunate we all are that this has nothing to do with music!" We can still honour and admire Rossini for his own creations, but it is a different matter when we realise that largely as a result of the critical writings of the time, the Paris Opera should have presented year after year new productions by a mediocre Meyerbeer, and almost nothing by Berlioz. The fact that Berlioz was himself such a perceptive and engaging music critic, somehow makes this even worse.

Any consideration of the role of the critic in the arts must therefore begin with what will hopefully be a brief survey of the history of art criticism.

What is amazing is that in any discussion of the arts, of art critics or of aesthetic theories, we still have to trail back five centuries before the birth of Christ to the achievements of the ancient Greeks. It is a truism to say that our culture began with those Athenian citizens, but as far as the arts are concerned, what they thought and wrote and created has clung like an Old Man of the Sea on to the shoulders of European art ever since. As we shall see, their refining of naturalism in the visual arts firmly directed the development of Western visual arts until well into the 20th century. In order to prove my point, let me come briefly forward to the early 18th century, to quote from a work originally written in Latin (that in itself speaks volumes about classical influence!), 'De Arte Graphica' by Du Fresnoy (1611-1688) translated into French by de Piles (1635-1709) and then translated into English by that distinguished poet and critic, John Dryden, and published in 1713 as 'The Art of Painting':

> 'The principal and most important part of Painting is to find out and thoroughly to understand what nature has made most beautiful and most proper to this Art; and that a choice of it may be made according to the Tastes and manner of the Ancients: Without which all is nothing but a blind and rash Barbarity; which rejects what is most beautiful and seems with audacious Insolence to despise an Art, of which it is wholly ignorant…Our business is to imitate the beauties of Nature as the Ancients have done before us, and as the Object and Nature of the thing require from us. And for this reason we must be careful in the Search of Ancient Medals, Statues, Gems,

Vases, Paintings and Basso-Relievos; And of all
other things which discover to us the Thoughts
and Inventions of the Graecians; because they
furnish us with great Ideas and make our
Productions wholly Beautiful.'

Dryden is writing 1200 years after the flowering of
ancient Greek culture, and yet is still slavishly kow-
towing to it. So what was it that made what they created
and what they thought and wrote about the arts so
special? The first thing to notice is that they did indeed
write and think about and discuss the role of the arts
in society. That in itself made them special and different. In Plato, in Aristotle, in Xenophon's reminiscences
of what Socrates said, we have an astonishing record of
well thought-out ideas about the role of arts. Although
they were surrounded by things made and being created
to give aesthetic pleasure, that whole concept would
have been alien to their thinking. That has probably
been the case since humankind first emerged. From the
making of clay pots, to hand axes, to the cave paintings of the Aurignacian and Magdalenian periods,
it is obvious that although what we call artefacts had
immediate social purposes, some of which we no longer
understand, a conscious effort has been made to make
them 'look as good as possible'. Pots have decoration
on them that is not strictly functional. Their propor-

tions may have been tapered to give a pleasing effect, and so on. The Greeks, like everybody before them, ignored this aspect of art. Adorno's 20th century theories about the autonomy of art, divorcing itself from its social purposes and social conditioning, to be enjoyed purely as a work which itself gives aesthetic pleasure, or theories of art for art's sake, would have been outside their comprehension altogether.

Ancient Greek art was very much a social art (or to use Adorno's terminology an instrumental art). It clearly met social purposes. It had a 'use'. It was part of social life. Poetry was written to be declaimed in public at every city or religious ceremony, not to be savoured in private. Often it was sung as part of the music which accompanied most social ceremonies. Reading and writing Homer were the bedrock of what they learned at school. Drama was part of a religious ceremony attended by all the citizens. Sculptures were made to adorn temples, or to commemorate a man's life. The Greeks had no idea of 'fine' arts. Indeed they had no word for art at all. Artefacts were judged according to how well they were made, and according to how well they met the purpose for which they were intended and whether that purpose was worthwhile. In Plato's dialogue, 'Hippias Major', he proposes a definition of beauty as 'effectiveness for some good purpose'.

Technique and educational, moral and social effectiveness were the criteria by which art was judged. Yet Plato was an idealist. He thought a glimpse of beauty was a glimpse of the ideal, the perfect, the divine.

The art they were judging was revolutionary. The Greeks, and the Romans after them, so refined the visual arts as to push them in a radically new direction, into forms which we call naturalism. Increasingly, artists tried to make a work seem more like real life. A sculpture might be made of marble or bronze, but its creator's aim was to make the figure it portrayed as lifelike as possible. Virgil in the 'Aeneid' (vi 847), describes 'gently breathing bronzes and faces that, though made in marble, were alive'. Using techniques of tone and perspective, painters too attempted to present a picture that was as close as possible to a representation of actual people, actual scenery, actual buildings. We still admire the skills they developed in doing so. E.H. Gombrich in 'Art and Illusion' (1960) stated, 'It needed the extension of our historical horizon and our increased awareness of the art of other civilizations to bring home to us what has rightly been called "the Greek miracle", the uniqueness of Greek art.' This move to naturalism in the visual arts was important because it flowered right through the classical period (and in the Roman Empire the arts became increasingly important from the Augustan age onwards) and, after the interregnum of the Dark Ages in northern Europe and the medieval period, flourished with growing confidence in Europe from the Renaissance until the invention of the camera in the 19th century halted it in its tracks. By then European culture had become so used to naturalism, that it almost took it for granted.

Yet as Harold Osborne has perceptively pointed out in his 'Aesthetics and Art Theory', naturalism had disadvantages, particularly for art critics. In a sense, a picture that is attempting to show people and scenery that are really 'out there' in actual life, pushes the viewer through its frame, almost as though he or she was looking through a window on the wall at what is real and actual. As a result the viewer and the critic tend to concentrate on the subject of the picture rather than on the picture itself. This has meant in practice that a great deal of art criticism has tended to be descriptive rather than analytical, tended to describe the subject of a picture rather than attempt to analyse the ways the painter has approached the problems of painting it. It is fair to say that what makes Gombrich such an excellent historian and art critic is precisely that he attempts to analyse the picture as a picture rather than be seduced by the painter into losing himself in the picture's subject matter. At the other extreme, André Malraux in his 'Les

Voix du Silence' (1951) has observed that Stendhal's voluminous account of the painter Correggio could be transferred almost without altering a word, to a description of a great actress on a stage in a theatre. Stendhal has stepped through the frame of the picture and is lost in the subject of the painting. Since most of the paintings of the ancient Greeks and Romans have perished, and all we have left is what was written about them, this is doubly distressing. We do not need the rhapsodising descriptions by Callistratus in the 4th century AD. What we would have liked would be some attempt to analyse what the painters and sculptors were trying to do, and how they were doing it.

In 1997, a fascinating exhibition, 'Ancient Faces: Mummy Portraits from Roman Egypt' at the British Museum, made it exhilaratingly clear that at least some paintings from the 2nd century AD had survived intact and these were put on show. Thanks to the exceptional preservative conditions of the Egyptian desert, they had been turning up in excavations throughout the 19th century, but art critics had paid them almost no attention. They fell into a gap between two scholarly specialisations. Egyptologists thought they were classical and Classicists thought they were Egyptian. From the 1st century AD onwards, Greek communities in Egypt under the Roman Empire had accepted Egyptian beliefs about mummification and the after-life, but added their own custom of including a portrait of the deceased's face on the outer case of the mummy. The ancient Greeks considered the high point of their painting tradition and heritage was reached under Apelles in the 4th century BC, but this tradition was obviously still flourishing in the Alexandrine School of painting from which the painters of the mummy cases came in the 2nd centuy AD. Some of the paintings were in tempera, some were in encaustic. Pliny in his 'Natural History' gives a recipe for Punic wax which recent experiments have proved to be an excellent painting medium that fits well with the evidence of the portraits. What was astonishing, and something of a revelation in this exhibition, was the dazzling range of skills and techniques apparent in the paintings themselves. They look amazingly modern. Not one of the range of skills and techniques naturalism prides itself on developing since the Renaissance is missing in these portraits. As Euphrosyne Dioxiadis wrote in the introduction to the catalogue, 'It is not until some fifteen centuries later, in the faces painted by Titian or Rembrandt's depiction of his own features as he saw them reflected in the mirror, that the same artistry ... is witnessed again.' These survivals, it should be remembered, came not from the big centres where it was all happening, not from Athens, Rome or even Alexandria, but from obscure provincial painters, competently maintaining a noble tradition.

It is depressing enough that in recent times, art critics and historians have ignored this astonishing array of talent as being outside their range of specialisation. What is even more depressing is the paltry evidence of what we want to know, provided in the writings of classical critics that have survived. Naturalism produced some wonderful art, but as Osborne made clear, it tended to reduce its art critics to rhapsodies of description of the subject matter of the paintings or the sculptures, not any worthwhile analysis of the works themselves.

There was one lively area of Greek art where naturalism played almost no part. This was the drama. This had developed a range of conventions of its own which took it far away from naturalism. It was written in verse, some of it sung by a chorus, or declaimed by masked figures. Nothing much actually happened on stage, since most of the action of the drama was reported as having happened off-stage. It tended to take place around one set of events, in one place and within a given timescale – the dramatic 'unities'. Bearing Osborne's observations in mind, it is not really surprising that it was around the drama, and also around public speaking which both the Greeks and the Romans considered an extremely important aspect of public life, that much important Greek and Roman art criticism centred.

Far and away the most important critic, indeed the first major critic as we understand the term, was Aristotle (384-322 BC). He was of course much more than that. He is still thought of as a major figure in the world of philosophy, logic and biology. Fortunately for posterity, this brilliant mind turned his attention to aesthetics, and to art criticism, and in the 'Poetics' incomplete as it is, and in the 'Rhetoric', he set out theories and insights, which to this day still colour our thinking, and which for better and for worse, dominated European assumptions about art, literature and drama for all too many centuries after his death.

From a modern point of view he had some limitations. He knew only ancient Greek literature and art as it existed in the 4th century BC. Like all Greeks of his time, he regarded all other cultures and civilisations around him as inferior and mere savagery. He was tutor to Alexander the Great, and we know that tensions grew between them when Alexander began to be fascinated by the Persian culture he was conquering. Much of the Greek literature and art that Aristotle knew has since perished, but we still have enough of ancient Greek literature, drama and art generally to know and share what made up Aristotle's knowledge and experience of art.

Since then we have advantages he did not have. Quite a bit has survived from the Roman period, so that we have at least a representative sample from the long and fruitful period of the Roman Empire's art and literature, about which he knew nothing at all. We also have the long creative achievements in Europe since the collapse of the Roman Empire, a long tradition which inevitably allows us to take a more comprehensive view, to say nothing of what we now know about other cultures throughout the world, including the Persian one of his own time which he so despised. Most of us would tend to side with Alexander.

Most of the literature he knew was in verse, much of it intended for performance in a theatre. It is understandable, given the drama of his day, that he should be rather dismissive of comedy, and pay more reverence to tragedy than later theatre history would justify. The glaring lack, from our point of view, is any substantial body of prose fiction. In prose he was limited to the works we still admire, Plato and Xenophon, Herodotus and Thucydides, and many of the great orators including Demosthenes.

Essentially the 'Poetics' concerns itself with poetry, and the 'Rhetoric', on the surface at least, deals with what was an important element in Greek life, the ability to speak well in public, 'speechcraft'; but in fact turns out to be in effect a careful analysis of the art of prose.

What is perhaps the most serious of Aristotle's limitations is the way ethics keeps crowding in on artistic judgements. While not as explicitly laid down as it is in his 'Metaphysics' or his 'Politics', Aristotle lays down solidly enough in the 'Poetics' and the 'Rhetoric' that the end of art is pleasure. Yet educational, moral and social effectiveness are always lurking in the background as part of any artistic judgement. In the theatre the audience was to be purged of suppressed emotions as well as pleased, and pleased in order to be purged. In prose the audience were to be pleased in order to be 'persuaded'. There was always the pill to be swallowed along with the sweetness of the pleasure. Here Aristotle's influence proved nothing short of disastrous, particularly in the 17th and 18th centuries.

Aristotle and Violence in the Media

Y ET HOW REFRESHING it is to find in the 'Poetics' carefully reasoned definitions and analysis. He first sets out his scheme for dealing with poetry, with its various kinds and their essential parts, the structure of the plot, the number and nature of the parts and the rest of the poetic method. Whether Epic, Tragedy, Comedy or Dithyrambic, poetry is essentially 'mimesis', an 'imitation' of life. But the different genres differ not only in the medium but in the aims and manner of that imitation. Having looked at music and dancing as non-literary examples of 'mimesis', he turns to poetry proper. After dealing with rhythm and metre and rhyme, he looks at the aims of poetry, to show men in action either as 'better than life' (heroic or idealising), 'as they are' (realistic naturalism) or 'worse' (caricature or satire). Poetry has two causes, the desire for imitation, with the pleasure that brings, and the desire for harmony. He says little on comedy, implying that he does not really warm to it. Epic and tragedy deserve more attention, tragedy above all others. Then he launches into the definition of tragedy that has been the basis for much speculation ever since.

Saintsbury translates it as 'An imitation of an action, serious, complete and possessing magnitude, in language sweetened with each kind of sweetening in the several parts, conveyed by action and recital, possessing pity and terror, accomplishing the purgation of such emotions.' It has become known as the theory of catharsis. Tragedy needs some thought as regards scenery, music and dancing, and the actual words, but it also requires 'consideration' and 'plot', the 'setting together of incidents', the 'action', to which 'character' is very much subordinate. Song is only a decoration (opera was centuries in the future) and scenery should come last of all since although influencing the soul, it is inartistic (this is presumably not a comment on theatre scenery in general but on the scenery available in 4th century Athens!). The plot has to be a complete whole with a beginning, a middle and an end. The plot must have unity, just so much and just so little so that there are no omissions and no redundancies. He then deals in detail with plot, character, consideration and the chorus. He then examines epic poetry and explains in detail why he thinks tragedy superior.

Among so much careful analysis, perhaps two ideas stand out: the theory of 'mimesis' and that of 'catharsis'. It is also worth noting that nowhere does he spell out the need for three dramatic unities as the seventeenth century critics insisted he did! Much has been hung on the peg of 'catharsis', the idea that much of the force of drama is that it enables the audience to act out in the theatre imaginatively passions and emotions that it therefore does not need to act out in real life. As the poet Milton puts it in his preface to 'Samson Agonistes', 'by raising pity and fear, or terror, to purge the mind of those and such-like passions – that is, to temper and reduce them to just measure with a kind of delight, stirred up by reading or seeing those passions well imitated'.

If one of his students had asked Aristotle for an example of catharsis in action, he might well have referred them to the play 'Agamemnon' by Aeschylus. Here Agamemnon, the overall commander of the Greeks during the ten years of the Trojan war, having finally destroyed Troy, returns home, only to discover, as so many soldiers returning from the wars have discovered, that his wife, Clytemnestra, has been having an affair with another man. He takes a bath while deciding what to do about this, but his wife forestalls him. While he is immersed in the calming water, she steals up behind him, throws a great cloak over him and hacks away at the writhing cloak with an axe, until it writhes no more, and blood seeps out from beneath the edges of the cloak. Agamemnon, who escaped the weapons of all the Trojans for so many years, could not escape those of his wife.

Now, however blissful the married state, there are moments of extreme irritation and exasperation, when most wives have a sudden, almost blinding desire to batter some sense into their uncomprehending spouses. Wives in general have the good sense to suppress these moments of fury. If there were wives in that 4th century Attic audience, Aristotle might say, they were able imaginatively to experience what it would be like to give way to these suppressed desires, and so work them out of their system. This would be catharsis in action. They would also, of course, work out the consequences too, looking at the terrible dilemma this posed for Clytemnestra's son Orestes, who was supposed both to honour and obey his mother and also avenge the death and restore the honour of his father.

Aristotle's theory has not been restricted to 4th century Athens. It is used extensively today to justify the depiction of violence in media fiction, particularly film and television. Fiction sets out to give a picture of real life. Violence is a part of real life. Fiction which ignored violence or falsified or sentimentalised it, would not be true to its role of imitating life. Depraved and deprived teenagers flock to films depicting horror and violence, we are told, just because they are able to work out of their system, urges which might otherwise lead them into anti-social acts which would have far more serious consequences than a mere visit to the cinema. Opponents deny this. On the contrary they say, this frequent depiction of so much violence, provides role models for them to imitate. No modern critic can afford to ignore this controversy.

Before immersing ourselves in these arguments, it might be as well to ask why people are so fascinated by violence anyway. The reason is fairly obvious. We are all frightened of being hurt, frightened of pain. It is a basic fear. When we were small, larger children could all too easily hurt us, and often did so. Even inanimate objects could suddenly turn against us, the stairs we were descending, the drawer we were trying to shut, could all too quickly turn to agony with a footstep put wrong, a finger left in the way. It is this basic fear of pain which underlies our fascination with violence. It is a fear that never goes away. The creators of film and television fiction know that if they depict violence and horror, they can plug into this basic fear and probably hold our fascinated attention very easily. That is why they have a responsibility to be true to life. If they are showing characters and a situation where violence would actually have arisen in real life, then it is surely fair to depict it in fiction. But if they are wallowing in violence for the sake of it, that might well be the moment when the responsible critic has to draw the line. 'Chainsaw Massacre Three' should not inspire confidence in the modern film critic, whatever Aristotle says.

There is also another process at work. Films showing horror and violence in the 1920s still exist and are still occasionally shown. In their day they left their audiences gripped and horrified. Nowadays they seem faintly comic and have almost no effect on us whatsoever. Why should this be so? Sadly, every film director making a film about violence knows that if his film is to be successful, if it is to put bums on seats (and in the film trade it is the number of tickets sold which matters, in television it is the ratings, the viewing figures that mean success or failure), he must make his violent scenes just that little bit more nauseating, more upsetting, than any film that has gone before him. Gradually, and it has been a slow process, this has meant that film audiences have been led down a primrose path of ever greater violence, ever more nauseating and upsetting nastiness. That is why the early films seem so ineffective. Modern audiences have become accustomed to much more sophisticated unpleasantness, so that violence has to be really horrid to evoke a response. Modern critics can rightly point out that this has raised the level of our expectations of violence, made it probably more likely that we opt for violence in real life as a result of what we have become accustomed to in the media. Aristotle's theory of catharsis still applies, but we have been drawn toward ever increasing violence and nastiness in the interests of making a profit and selling seats, something Aristotle could not possibly have foreseen. In his day entrance to the theatre was free!

Later Greek Critics, particularly Longinus

Sadly the later centuries of ancient Greek art criticism concerned themselves with endlessly refining the theories of Plato, Aristotle and others, inventing ever more complicated terms and categories, and splitting more and more philosophic hairs, until the process seemed to have become a positive maze of complexity, still concerning themselves chiefly with the public art of oratory. Modern readers may find French structuralist critics of the 1960s and 1970s heavy going, but here is a fairly typical example of 1st century AD Greek criticism from the fourth chapter of the third book of Hermogenes, a manual which became the textbook for later Greek rhetoric:

> Since many have set out many things about epicheiremes and have spent much speech on this, and nobody has been able to bring it home to the mind clearly, I shall endeavour, as clearly as I can, to decide what is the invention of the epicheireme which constructs the kephalaion or the lusis, and what the invention of the ergasia

which constructs the epicheireme and what the invention of the enthymeme which constructs the ergasia.

Pity the poor ancient Greek student of rhetoric!

There is one glorious exception, 'Longinus on the Sublime.' We know surprisingly little about him, and it is only by amazing luck that his treatise has survived at all. In the 10th century it was copied into a medieval manuscript, although it has been estimated that about a third of the treatise is lost. What we have is so valuable as to make this loss even more regrettable. The treatise appears to date from the 1st century AD. It quotes from over fifty writers, none of them later than the 1st century. We have no reference to Longinus in any writer of antiquity, but then his treatise is a response to and a rebuttal of another work on the Sublime by one Caecilius. We have no reference to him either by any writer in antiquity. It is a sad reminder of how much we have lost from the intellectual life of so many hundreds of years in the classical period. There can be no doubt of the work's authenticity, since, fortunately for us, it quotes in full a poem by Sappho, the 'Ode to Anactoria', which would otherwise have been completely lost. All too many of its other references have been lost also. The work was published in Basle in 1559, but it was Boileau's 1674 translation into French which established its importance in France, as did William Smith's 1739 English translation in England. It had a considerable influence on Edmund Burke, and was an important influence on Romanticism. It is astonishing that a work written in the 1st century should have proved so relevant, and so much admired, more than 1700 years after it was written.

What made it so special? The first thing to notice is that the word 'sublime' is not a very good translation. 'The best and finest' might be a closer approximation to the meaning the word had for Longinus. In one way, he can be thought of as the first of the 'moderns'. He brushes aside all talk of the social value of the work of art, and is not concerned with whether art helps us purge our emotions, extends our imaginative experience of life, or is morally improving. Nor is he bothered about 'persuading' an audience. He comes straight out and says firmly and without equivocation that art exists to give us 'transports of delight', and it succeeds or fails purely in terms of whether it manages to do this or not. This is the first clear statement of A.E. Houseman's 'bristling at the back of the neck', that clear and unmistakeable wave of pleasure that art can bring. He is only concerned with literature, but boldly sets out to analyse what makes for the sublime. He defines five sources, command of strong and manly thought; grandly felt passions; skill at manipulating figures of speech; brilliant language; and admirable composition. He gives a fine range of examples to prove each point he makes, although sadly, in all too many cases, we no longer know the works he mentions.

Roman Critics

THE ROMAN CRITICS, foremost among them those who devoted themselves to literature like Horace, Cicero and above all Quintilian, although ready to compare Homer with Virgil, often to the benefit of the latter, remained a little too awe-struck by the achievements of the Greeks, to reach any real independence. With the doubtful exception of the Satire, the Romans created no new literary forms, even their theatre was a pretty slavish imitation of the Greeks, unless one includes the brutalities of arenas like the Colosseum, which do not exactly redound to their credit.

Yet the savouring of the finest examples of the different arts, comparisons between them, discussions about them and attempts to analyse their effects and creative workmanship, were all something the classical period increasingly took for granted as part of social intercourse among educated people. All this and so much more were swept away in the collapse of the Roman Empire in the West and the disintegration and poverty of what historians call the Dark Ages which followed that collapse in the 5th and 6th centuries AD. Only as society gradually stabilised and reorganised itself in

Europe in what historians call the Medieval Period did the arts, haltingly and in very different circumstances, begin to matter once again.

The Middle Ages

THE MIDDLE AGES, stretching from the 8th to the 15th centuries, now seem strangely alien to modern eyes. Poverty, ignorance and superstition were the background to deeply felt religious faith. At the same time we can only admire some of the social values of the time. Charging interest on a loan was felt to be 'taking an advantage of others less well placed', and therefore unfair. Charging more for something than it was worth was felt to be a crime that should be punished. Paying less than fair wages to workers was also punishable by law. The Church went out of its way to support and help those who were sick or disabled. Society made a positive effort to be 'fair' to its members. The market economy existed only as a pale shadow of what it would eventually become.

In medieval society, the arts were handmaidens to religion, their purpose being to help the Church to spread the word of God. Not all the arts were so high-minded. Popular music, songs and ballads tended to develop themes the Church did not approve of. Performing troops of mime players seem to have continued to tour widely from classical times onwards, performing in fairs and market places. Much of the proof they were there at all depends on the frequent attempts by the church to have them banned altogether. Their subject matter depended on bawdiness and farmyard humour which the Church did not like at all. They were still there in the Renaissance, by then calling themselves the Commedia dell'Arte.

The queen of the arts was undoubtedly architecture. It dominated the other arts. Sculpture and painting were there to adorn the churches and cathedrals. Furniture and even jewellery did their best to pretend they were really architecture. One of the many ironies of the Albert Memorial in Hyde Park, designed and built in the white heat of the 19th century's Gothic Revival, is that it was based on miniature medieval shrines, that were doing their best to pretend they were really architecture, until Sir George Gilbert Scott came along and transformed them into real architecture, from fantasy to reality, with stunning effect. Similarly, the anonymous architects and builders who laboriously erected the magnificent cathedrals we still cherish, would never have guessed that the buildings they spent their lives creating to the greater glory of God, would one day be appreciated and savoured in their own right as superb works of art.

Art critics were in very short supply during the medieval period. The historian has to rely when attempting to estimate what people thought about art, on picking up views expressed while the writers were mainly talking about something else. There is one illustrious exception. At the beginning of the 14th century, the greatest poet of the period, Dante himself, wrote a treatise in Latin, 'De Vulgari Eloquentia', defending the use of the vernacular, everyday Florentine Italian, for the poetry he was so magnificently creating, and discussing in detail what made poetry effective as an art form. It might seem contradictory to write in Latin how important it was not to write in Latin, but that is how the Middle Ages were. Latin was the common language among an educated minority right across Europe. It obviously helped to create a widespread cosmopolitanism, a sense that being European was as important as being whatever particular nationality an individual claimed. Dante intelligently and comprehensively surveys the main divisions of European languages, and understandably plumps for his own Florentine version of Italian. He seems not to know very much of the many hundreds of years of classical Greek and Roman criticism that preceded the Dark Ages. He clearly knows a great deal less of them than we do today. He has not read the 'Poetics' of Aristotle, he has not read Longinus on the Sublime. In a sense he is starting from scratch. It is clear that for him, criticism involves looking at the ways a writer chooses to express his ideas, and the impression this makes on the reader, and he proceeds, robustly, to look at the kinds of poetic diction available to the poet in the vernacular. It is a brilliant discussion from a man of genius. It therefore goes almost without saying, that it was largely ignored in his own time and has been generally undervalued since.

A good example of the kind of detective work the art historian has to do to try and find out what people thought of art in this long and fascinating period is provided by a late 14th century Lollard work, 'A Treatise of Miraclis Playinge'. The early Christian Church, after originally banning any kind of drama, eventually came round to seeing that drama, like painting and sculpture, could be used to try and convey the Christian message to an illiterate, superstitious and ignorant congregation. Throughout the Middle Ages drama became steadily more organised and more important. It developed into two kinds, drama played out in an arena, generally specially built for the occasion, and street drama, where a succession of carts, each showing a scene in the play, trundled round a city, to assembled groups of spectators, playing the same scene over and over to different groups. The players had to be local amateurs, speaking a dialect the audience understood, but the production was organised by the Church in conjunction with the local craft guilds, generally overseen by itinerant priests who specialised in putting on shows of this kind. The Middle English Dictionary defines 'miracle' as 'A dramatisation of any Scriptural event or legend of a saint, martyr etc. also a performance of such a play'. The Lollard author is therefore concerning himself with what was fairly typical of town life in the medieval period, the presentation of a play. He is critical because he considers a play 'trivial', whereas a religious truth is serious and not to be taken lightly. A play breaks the second commandment because (and I have updated some of the language) 'no man should use in bawdiness and play, the miracle and works that Christ so earnestly wrought for our health.' This is, as David Mills in the 'Revels History of Drama' points out, the exact opposite of Chaucer's 'and eek men shall nat maken ernest of game', but the sense that 'game' is trivial and not to be taken seriously, whereas religion belongs to what one should be very serious about, is clear enough. The ancient Greeks could laugh about what they took seriously, and Chaucer is civilised enough to do the same, but the Lollard author sees things in black and white. Laughter was trivial and religion was serious, and never the twain shall meet.

He looks at the arguments used in favour of religious drama; that they teach the Bible stories and help in spreading devotion. Clearly this was a stock defence. Friar William Melton used it to praise the York Corpus Christi play of 1426 :

> Also profitable to men and to the worship of God is to fulfil and seek all the means by which men leave sin and draw themselves to virtue. And just as there are men who only by earnest good works will be converted to God, so there are other men that will not be converted to God except by recreation and play

Our author denies that this is possible. Plays cannot convert men for they are themselves untrue when compared to the actual words of scripture. They are created, 'more to delight bodily desires than to be a book to guide lewd men.' They create only the illusion of being sorry for evil acts, by appealing to physical senses and desires, 'and therefore, being more sorry for pain than sin, they falsely weep for a loss of bodily prosperity, rather than for the loss of truly spiritual things.' Since many of the miracle plays enacted the painful martyrdom of saints, with much use of 'pigges blood' and firecrackers, one can see that the Lollard author had a point. Plays may look like a form of worship, but they are different from real devotion and teaching, both in the way they appeal and in the response they evoke.

This brings our author to his most telling point. He realises that drama exists as drama, and that religious drama just happens to be about religion, with an ostensibly religious aim and subject matter. But its real aim is different. It is trying to create effective drama. The priests who stage drama are looking for what works best on the audience as they watch the action, and they are working hard not so much to convert the spectators as to make the drama as effective as possible for that moment.

These miracle players and their supporters are veritable apostates; both because they put God behind them and give priority to their own lusts. They have God in mind only for the sake of the play, and they delight far more in the play than in the miracle it supposedly deals with.

He goes on to make a comparison between the preacher and the play. Often their subject matter is the same. The preacher in the pulpit can be very dramatic, using many of the tricks that an actor uses. But the preacher hopefully practises what he preaches (has our author read Chaucer?) whereas our author has some scathing things to say about the real lives of those who act in plays and about the mercenary motives of many of those who support them, and he questions the behaviour and the motives of all too many in the audience as well.

I have devoted space to this Lollard partly because he is the authentic voice of medieval criticism (and not so very different from Bible belt, Mid-Western 21st century America!) but more because he is typical of all too many critics in that he is depressingly unaware of where his own arguments lead. The Middle Ages had no word for drama, but he is effectively clearing ground away to establish drama as a separate art form, as a genre in its own right. He recognises that particular and unique excitement that good drama can set up between actors and audience in a theatre. In effect he is recognising that he is dealing with an art, but he condemns it because it is not propaganda. Aristotle accepted that drama gave pleasure, but felt it also had social purposes as well. The Lollard regards pleasure as sinful, and denies that drama can be a useful propaganda for religion. All the same he is teetering on the edge of admitting that as an art form it brings 'transports of delight', although nothing would allow him to admit that might be the sole justification for the whole process. He is opposed to drama root and branch, but his own argument could almost be used to justify and defend the very thing he sets out to condemn.

The Renaissance

T HE MEDIEVAL PERIOD is followed in the 15th and 16th centuries by what historians call the Renaissance. By any standards this was a time of radical change, a ferment of new ideas, values and assumptions, brought about by a combination of surprising developments. The final collapse of the classical Eastern Empire with the fall of Constantinople to the Turks in 1453, followed by the apparent threat of an Islamic invasion of Western Europe, had a sobering effect, even if followed a generation later by the final expulsion of the Moors from Spain. The brilliant work by the Arabs in preserving and translating classical texts in Toledo, which gradually permeated through intellectual centres in Europe, was reinforced by the material fleeing scholars from Constantinople brought with them. 'Renaissance' is a French word meaning 'rebirth', and a renewed interest in classical texts and culture became a primary force in the Renaissance. The invention of printing, and the increasing availability of texts and translations, greatly facilitated this process. The discovery of America, and of the sea route to the Far East, aroused a spirit of adventure and exploration, and a general widening of horizons. Moves to reform the Church, and the rise of Protestantism in Northern Europe, did much to lift the strangle-hold with which the Church had so long gripped society. As Froude put it, "In the fabric of habit which they had so laboriously built for themselves, men could remain no longer."

Modern science, started by the ancient Greeks fearlessly asking rational questions and expecting rational answers, slowly picked up the shattered pieces of its destruction by the medieval clergy and pulled itself together all over again. Galileo (1564-1642) invented the first astronomical telescope in 1609 and, peering at the heavens, discovered that the Church's account had got it wrong. The Church fought back. On the Pope's orders, Galileo was taken down to view the instruments of torture, and the frightened man understandably recanted and disavowed all he had previously maintained. Yet as Milton's 'Areopagitica' would later assert, ideas are not defeated by force, they are defeated by better ideas. The centre and focus of modern science moved to northern Europe, where freedom to argue about ideas was becoming more easily established.

Northern Europe benefited too from the weakening of Venice, which during the Middle Ages had become Europe's gateway to the lucrative trade in luxury goods and much needed spices from the East along the Silk

Road. The Turks closed off this access to the East just as Europe's sailors were discovering America and exploring the African coast with its future possibilities of a profitable slave trade. Italy's loss became a gain for Spain and Portugal and, later, Holland, France and England. Increasing stability, prosperity and productivity, with trading interests becoming ever more important, ensured that a merchant class, growing in influence and status, pushed more and more stridently for the advantages of the free market economy, as opposed to the strictly controlled economy of the medieval era (an economy originally controlled in the interests of everybody, not one organised so that entrepreneurs could make a great deal of money at other people's expense!).

Bound up with this process were the fortunes of the lay rulers, the kings, princes, dukes and counts, who throughout the medieval period had often found themselves in conflict with the Church and had almost invariably lost the fight. The Church had the ultimate weapon of excommunication in its armoury, which if used, meant the ruler's subjects no longer had to obey him and, if pushed, the Church did not hesitate to use it. The Protestant Reformation changed all that. The ruler became steadily more powerful than the Church. Pope Pius V did indeed excommunicate England's Queen Elizabeth in 1570, but to remarkably little effect.

It is not surprising that in the midst of all this revolt, rebellion and changing attitudes and assumptions, the role of criticism and the critic should have become increasingly influential. A new figure, the educated humanist, appeared on the intellectual scene, and became steadily more dominant. Figures like Erasmus (1466-1536) did much to establish a new approach to the individual and to society amidst often violent and bigoted religious controversy.

Humanism Under Attack

P ARADOXICALLY, HUMANISTS FOUND themselves under attack from an unexpected quarter. The very Protestantism which they themselves had in some ways been responsible for setting in motion, turned against some of their cherished beliefs. Extreme Protestantism had no time for art, much less art criticism. The very idea that art could bring pleasure, much less the 'transports of delight' that the text of Longinus, now available in print, suggested, was nothing short of anathema to puritans like Calvin (1509-1564). Indulging in pleasure for its own sake was sinful, and the puritans condemned it out of hand. It is therefore understandable that much early art criticism in the Renaissance should have depended heavily on the newly influential writings of Plato and Aristotle to produce a defence of art in terms of its social significance and usefulness. Art was defended as being 'educational', as 'broadening horizons' and 'making people better'. 16th century Italian art critics like Scaliger, Castelvetro or Tasso, because Italy was in advance of the rest of Europe in the Renaissance, and 17th century French critics like Malherbe, Saint-Evremond and Boileau, as France gradually became the arbiter of Europe, all adopted this view of art. It should be realised that they were in a sense a beleaguered garrison, beset with Puritan attackers, defending what they most believed in. In Adorno's terms, this is the 'instrumental' view of art. It has had many more recent defenders, notably Leo Tolstoy in his book, 'What is Art?' published in 1898. He said 'It is necessary for a society in which works of art arise and are supported to find out whether all that professes to be art really is art; whether (as is presupposed in our society) all that which is art is good; and whether it is important and worth those sacrifices which it necessitates.' He believed he had found the social function of art and so its justification. 'Art is a human activity consisting in this, that one man consciously, by means of external signs, hands on to others feelings he has lived through, and that other people are infected by these feelings and also experience them.' Good art transmitted to others by means of this 'infection', 'the highest and best feelings to which men have arisen'.

It is worth noting, as Harold Osborne has done in 'Aesthetics and Art Theory', that genuine aesthetic appreciation is not bound up with a direct emotional response. One of the many things works of art may well do is arouse emotion, but the aesthetic response to a work of art is different from the emotional response to a

Midwest American fundamentalist sermon, or political oratory. Nowadays, bearing in mind Adorno's theories of autonomous art, Tolstoy is thought to have missed the point, concentrating on the social effects of art and not on what art is really about; and so did the 16th century Italian and the 17th century French critics.

Two New Art Forms

Y ET THIS RENEWED interest in classical Greek and
Roman culture did, among other advantages, have
at least two unexpectedly splendid results. Without
really intending to, the Renaissance invented two new
art forms – opera and ballet. Most of the credit must
go to the art critics and historians who had prepared
the way. 'Historicism', a preoccupation, almost an
obsession with the glories of the past, became a part
of Italian critics' ideology throughout the Renaissance.
It pervaded painting, sculpture, literature and architecture. We have already noted it in Dryden as late as
the 1690s. Inevitably the whole area of classical drama
fascinated Italian critics and historians too. Throughout
Europe, students in schools and universities put on
plays based on the texts of Plautus, Terence and Seneca.
Sadly, whereas Arab scholars in Toledo and elsewhere
had faithfully translated and preserved many Greek
and Latin texts, Arab culture had no theatres and so
the Arabs largely ignored and failed to preserve Greek
drama. Fortunately, from Constantinople and elsewhere, full texts from Aeschylus, Euripedes, Sophocles
and Aristophanes survived to give a sufficient picture

of some of the glories of Greek drama. Spurred on by Italian art critics, the dream arose of recreating the glories of Athens and Rome, of restaging some of the masterpieces of Greek drama as they might have looked and in the kind of theatre they were first written for. Groups of critics, intellectuals and art lovers, like the Camerata in Florence, pooled their hopes, ideas and positive intentions.

A reproduction of a classical Roman theatre, the 'Teatro Olympico' with a permanent architectural stage set was carefully erected in Vicenza (1580-5). Another was built in Sabionetta in 1590 and yet another in Parma in 1619. This last, built of wood, and fortunately protected from the weather by being enclosed within a larger hall, the 'Farnese', has happily survived to the present, and although damaged in World War II, it has been carefully restored. We know a great deal more about classical theatre than they did in 1580, but what mattered was that here was a deliberate attempt to recreate the classical theatre as they thought it had been. Imposed on the Italian theatre from above, by a mixture of critics nostalgic for former glories, intellectuals, scholars, and aristocrats anxious to show off their importance by cashing in on new ideas about drama, this attempt to revive the past took some surprisingly new directions and ended up, almost by accident, creating two altogether fresh forms of drama.

Those well-informed Italian critics in the 16th century knew that Greek drama had involved music, with singing and dancing. If they were to restage the texts that had survived they would need music, singing and dancing too. Unfortunately nobody had any idea what ancient Greek music, singing and dancing had actually been like. Attempts at restaging had therefore boldly to invent what had been lost. Even more excitingly they must have thought, would it not be challenging to attempt to write, compose, design and choreograph plays in the old manner, to take up where the Greeks and Romans had left off and so carry on a great tradition?

What they were circling around was in fact a kind of musical theatre; a mixture of music, spectacle, acting, drama, singing and dancing. What is surprising, looking at what actually developed, is how quickly singing and dancing seemed to separate off from each other. After all if we dash forward in time and look at the development of the American 'musical' in American theatre, it cheerfully combined singing and dancing without a second thought. Its gifted performers, like Fred and Adele Astaire, spoke, acted, sang and danced with impressive ease.

The reasons for the difference were probably to be found in Italy's long tradition of church singing. Most modern males would agree with alacrity that it was better not to be a medieval choirboy with a very beautiful voice. The Church then had no qualms about castrating boys in order to preserve the beauty of their voices. Sex was generally considered a sinful activity, and as St Paul had long ago laid down in his First Epistle to the Corinthians, 'It is good for a man not to touch a woman'. Priests were supposed to avoid all temptation and remain untouched by the lusts of the flesh. Castrating a boy was to remove him from many of the devil's most cunning temptations, and what could be nobler than spending a castrated life singing to the greater glory of God? If modern males think otherwise, it is because they no longer share the medieval mindset, even if they have managed to keep their testicles intact.

Eunuchs tend to get fat. In addition to this both male and female singers tend to need a large diaphragm and so tend to have a large everything else. Over hundreds of years of choral and solo singing, the Church had pushed the training of singers' voices almost as far as it could go, so it was in the nature of things that outstanding singers who could tackle the kind of music that composers like Caccini (1551-1618), Peri (1561-1633) and Monteverdi (1567-1643) wrote for them, would have been on the weighty side. No doubt they sang beautifully, but if they had been asked to dance, their elephantine cavortings might well have been too much even for the sturdy wooden stage of the 'Teatro Olympico'.

I am well aware that modern voice training and opera singers have greatly changed the image of opera for the better, but even when I first started opera–going, some enormous female, at whose bosom one could only gaze in horrified conjecture, would waddle on to the stage, followed by an equally large male, with his adipose tissue wobbling in all directions, and with a paunch that reached almost to his knees. This would make his attempt to kneel before her very much a triumph of mind over matter. He would then take her meat-slab of a hand in his and sing 'Your tiny hand is frozen!' It required a considerable imaginative effort on the part of the audience to make the necessary allowances. I was always amazed that the music critics of the day were so ready to make allowances too. Obviously the music and singing came first, but sometimes drama and spectacle seemed not to matter at all. Nowadays, opera audiences can sometimes be even more baffled by sets and costumes, which although wildly imaginative, can seem to have almost nothing to do with what is actually going on in the drama at all. And opera critics can seem almost equally prepared to make allowances still!

As a result, 'opera seria', telling a serious story based on classical mythological legends, its formal music rooted in madrigals, often with a leading role for a 'castrato', either had no dance element, or if it did, used a different set of performers for the dance. Understandably the dancers, not to be outdone and unable to compete with the weighty singers, developed a form of story telling that dispensed with singers altogether and told the story in gesture and dance. The origins of these two art forms, opera and ballet, were to be found in these late 16th and early 17th century performances, yet the Italian critics, intellectuals and aristocrats who fostered them had no idea what their efforts would bring forth. Their aim was to revive the ancient glories of Greece and Rome. Ballet's status in the 18th century was greatly helped by the emergence of an outstanding choreographer, who also wrote and theorised brilliantly about his chosen art form. Garrick thought him the 'Shakespeare of the dance'. Jean-Georges Noverre's 'Lettres sur La Danse' is a book still read and admired by ballet enthusiasts to this day.

France's Golden Age

U NDER LOUIS XIV, 17th century France enjoyed a golden age, admired and imitated by the rest of Europe, which it dominated politically, militarily and culturally. Particularly in the second half of the century, its leading artists set a standard, not only for France, but for the rest of Europe too. This makes it all the more infuriating that art criticism, even literary criticism (because after all most critics have to write) should seem so baffling for us. There were plenty of people writing animatedly and well about music, architecture, painting, sculpture, plays, novels and poetry in the seventeenth century. Yet by our standards they were too blinkered to be thought of as critics. Blinkered because they accepted basic presumptions and grounded their views largely upon them, which we can no longer share.

Firstly they were convinced that the purpose of art was to do good, to leave ordinary humans morally better after experiencing it than they were before. Art's job was seen therefore as somehow to sweeten the moral pill so that it could be swallowed with pleasure and enjoyment. Aristotle had laid down a set of guidelines by which this could be achieved and to ignore them was to court disaster and failure. Critics, when faced with a work of art, asked first what moral improvement resulted from experiencing it, and then to what extent it had achieved its ends by following the guidelines laid down in antiquity. Since we no longer ask these questions, the answers 17th century critics produced so copiously, seem to us curiously dated and irrelevant, but they mattered a great deal at the time. They hampered and made almost impossible any worthwhile discussion of what artists were actually trying to do. Indeed by modern standards the period is remarkable for the range and splendour of artistic creations which it never seemed capable of understanding or fully appreciating. Art critics must bear a heavy share of the responsibility for a sadly uninformed audience as result. Here is the distinguished playwright of the period, Pierre Corneille, on the difficulty of trying to present a French version of Sophocles' 'Oedipus':

> I realised that what a previous era had thought miraculous, would be too upsetting for our own. The unlikely and well-spoken part where he pushes the bronze pins into his own eyes and blinds himself, taking up most of Act V, would not suit the tender feelings of the ladies in my audience, and their hostility would spread to others. And as a final remark, there being no

love affair, the play is missing what the audience want most. So I have avoided what is offensive, and brought in an affair of the heart between Theseus and Dirce.

One can almost hear a Cecil B. DeMille-like Hollywood film producer saying 'This business of putting out his own eyes, I mean that's too gruesome for this classy kind of film, and where's the love interest? You gotta have love interest. What about this Theseus guy? Couldn't he and Dirce maybe…?'

So one of the great tragedies of ancient Greek theatre had to be sentimentalised almost out of existence to please the ladies. I am sure feminists would be outraged if anybody uses this as an argument for suggesting that perhaps women were not admitted to ancient Greek theatre audiences, still a matter of academic controversy!

Corneille's 'Oedipe' was one of the theatre successes of 1659. Only a generation earlier in England, Shakespeare could, with impunity, have the Duke of Gloucester's eyes put out on stage, for an audience that certainly included women as well as men, even if they were in a minority. Sophocles after all only has Oedipus' horrifying action reported as taking place off stage, although even that was too much for Corneille's audience. Shakespeare did not have entrenched, influential and self-important drama critics to deal with. Corneille, Moliere and Racine did. To be fair, although the puritans vigorously attacked the theatre in Shakespeare's time, they occupied nothing like the powerful position the Roman Catholic Church occupied so strenuously in France under Louis XIV, and the Church invariably pushed itself into the centre of most controversies over drama in this period.

Art Critics Harm the Theatre

Y ET IT WAS the literary critics who managed to do the theatre incalculable harm in the next two centuries. In the 17th century the words 'poet' and 'playwright' were almost interchangeable. If one was a creative writer, one wrote for the theatre. Drama played a central role in the culture. This was not to last. In England the Civil War between Cavaliers and Roundheads resulted in the victory of the puritans. Charles I was executed and a dictatorship eventually established under Oliver Cromwell. Theatre – all theatre – was banned from 1642-1660. A whole generation grew up without theatre. When Charles II was restored to the throne in 1660, theatre returned, but it was a different kind of theatre, drama written and enjoyed by an aristocratic minority, rather than by the much broader cross section of the community who crowded in to see Shakespeare's plays. Increasingly the great majority of what might have been the theatre-going public, became suspicious of drama. They distrusted it. They saw theatre as basically flawed, immoral in ways that bit much deeper than mere sexually licentious shocks and alarms. Drama was generally seen to be bad for everybody.

This was still the case when Jane Austen published 'Mansfield Park' in 1814. Edward Said in his 'Culture and Imperialism', makes much of the visit of Sir Thomas Bertram to Antigua in this very novel, as an example of the way England's upper class depended increasingly for its wealth on colonial exploitation. One has to look very hard for clues about this in the novel itself. What will strike most modern readers is an astonishing attitude to the theatre. Sir Thomas, a man of considerable personal integrity at home, whatever his wealth is based on, visits Antigua. While he is away (and journeys then took many months), the young adults of his family decide to indulge in amateur theatricals and amuse the neighbourhood with the performance of a play. When preparations are well advanced, Sir Thomas unexpectedly returns. Everybody accepts that the play cannot take place, that the idea of its performance is morally unsound, and most of them feel ashamed of themselves. The reader of the novel is clearly expected to concur. Modern readers can do nothing of the kind. There is a gap – more than a gap, a chasm – between attitudes in 1814 and ourselves. Jane Austen is clearly convinced, as were the majority of her readers, of the rightness of her views. Are we then so very different from the 'weltanschaung', the zeitgeist, the ideology of a mere two centuries ago? Even more importantly, where did this educated consensus of 1814 come from, so different from that of the courtiers of James 1 crowding in to see a royal performance of Shakespeare's company (the King's men!) or from the courtiers of Charles 1 crowding in to see a masque by Ben Jonson, designed by Inigo Jones, or from the audience, say, for Milton's 'Comus'?

Theatre's decline in the 18th century was paralleled by the rise of the novel. By 1780 the novel, not the play, had become the dominant art form for fiction. 18th century French critics credited England with the invention of the novel. It was greatly helped on its way by the introduction in 1737 of censorship in the theatre. Henry Fielding's play 'Tom Thumb' (1730) and other successful satires on the government and monarchy, persuaded the then prime minister, Robert Walpole, that plays and indeed theatres, should be licensed and controlled. London was officially restricted to two theatres, at Covent Garden and Drury Lane, and plays written after 1737 had to be licensed by the Lord Chamberlain. The effect of this was to drive many good writers out of the theatre. Henry Fielding was himself a sad example. The man who went on to write those much admired novels, 'Joseph Andrews', 'Tom Jones' and 'Amelia', had started as a successful playwright. He ended as one of our distinguished novelists, opting out of a controlled and censored theatre and choosing the adventurous challenge of a new and rapidly developing art form.

Yet surely fiction was fiction, fantasy was fantasy, and imagining characters in the novel was not so very different from, and was indeed an extension of, what had been done so honourably and for so many centuries in the theatre?

Not so! And for a very curious ambivalence in attitudes to the drama as opposed to the novel, we have to thank some very influential and wrong headed critics. The moral opprobrium that descended in stifling folds on the theatre, did not apply to the novel. Jane Austen herself in 'Northanger Abbey', a delicious satire on the new gothic horror novels of her day, which at one level is an ironic attack on the power of the media to change public attitudes and assumptions, managed to make great claims for the art of the novel. Perhaps she has her fluent tongue lodged a little in her gifted cheek, but there is a serious strand in what she tells her readers. Novels are where 'the greatest powers of the mind are displayed, in which the most thorough knowledge of human nature, the happiest delineation of its varieties, the liveliest effusions of wit and humour are conveyed to the world in the best chosen language.'

We should remember this is from the very self same writer who expects her readers to condemn out of hand the cheerful little enterprise of an amateur performance of 'Lovers' Vows'. The paradox is that Jane Austen and her readers all went to the theatre as a matter of course. The fashionable society she describes in Bath for its 'season', spent a great deal of time at the theatre. Indeed the very theatre they went to so assiduously is still there, still functioning as a working theatre, and still giving pleasure to its audiences. The difference is that a modern audience does not feel slightly guilty about going there. The nearest modern equivalent would be attitudes to a gambling casino. The majority of people tend not to go to casinos, and those who do, even if they have the luck to rake in winnings, feel vaguely ashamed of themselves. They know that gambling is morally unsound. That is how people felt in the 18th and 19th centuries about theatre. More and more of them went, but they still had vague feelings they should not. Astonishingly these attitudes persisted even as theatre gradually became more respectable. The poet, Alfred Lord Tennyson, one of the most popular, well loved and respected public figures of his day, wrote plays that were put on by the leading Victorian actor, Sir Henry Irving, the first actor to be knighted and made respectable, who played the leading role in Tennyson's plays. Yet Tennyson's wife, although devoted to him, would not have dreamed of going to the theatre to see her husband's plays put on. The theatre was no place for a respectable Victorian lady. Where did these assumptions come from?

Puritans and the Theatre

U NDOUBTEDLY PART OF the blame lay with the puritans. For them the only book was the Holy Bible, and the very idea of putting on a theatrical performance was to commit blasphemy. For some puritans it was a sin even to smile. It was these extreme puritan sects who triumphed in the English Civil War, cut off the head of Charles I and closed down the theatres altogether in 1642. Many of these same puritan sects left England in disgust at the Restoration in 1660, when the monarchy was restored by popular demand, the theatres opened again, and life tried to return to normal. They went to British colonies in America, and set up depressingly puritan societies there. (Anyone who disagrees should look at the Salem Witch trials.) They had managed to destroy a whole tradition of popular theatre-going in England in one generation. They were equally determined that no such tradition would be established in America. The theatre in their eyes was nothing but the work of the devil. The first permanent British settlement in America occurred at Jamestown, Virginia in 1607, followed by the better known arrival of the pilgrims at Plymouth Rock in New England in 1620. Yet there is no evidence of any professional theatre in the American colonies at all throughout the 17th century. In Accomac County, Virginia in 1665, three young men were hauled into court accused of actually having acted in a play. How scandalised Accomac County must have been at such impious behaviour! The court, no doubt reflecting British justice in the home country, was surprisingly lenient, and they were found 'not guilty of fault'. Nothing in British law should have prevented them from getting together to act out a play. The fact that they were taken to court and charged at all speaks volumes about American colonists' attitudes at the time. American prejudice remained surprisingly similar throughout the 18th century. In 1778, Congress passed a resolution condemning theatre-going and forbidding any person holding office under the United States to take part in or to encourage or to attend such abominations (the British Army had of course established theatres wherever they went). That very evening Lafayette invited General Washington to go to the theatre with him, and poor Washington, who like most British army officers, loved the theatre, had to refuse!

There were plenty of puritans left in England after 1660, and their prejudices did much to discredit the revival and increasing popularity of theatre-going in

England, but there were other, and if anything even more powerful, influences hostile to the theatre.

Critics Despise the Theatre

S ADLY, ONE OF the commonest sins committed by critics is to praise up one art form by decrying and devaluing another. An obvious example is the way opera and ballet have long puffed themselves up by sneering at each other. In 18th century France, still then the arbiter of European taste, there was a tendency to over-praise the novel by knocking the drama. There is a depressing gap between Jean-Jacques Rousseau's views on the novel and the drama. In 1758 Rousseau attacked Alembert's suggestion that a theatre should be set up in the republic of Geneva. Rousseau regarded theatre as a snare. Aristotle's theory of catharsis was a mere excuse for indulging in unhealthy feelings – unhealthy because they were false, all pretence and illusion. Actors were liars, pretending to be what they are not. Audiences lost themselves in the false emotions of others, so they fragmented their own identity and imaginatively took on false ones. Sexual morality was also put at risk by the abandoned behaviour of actresses.

Against these recitals of vice, Rousseau set the virtues of the novel. It was an English art form he thought, because the English were different from the French.

They were not constantly trying to win the approval of others, playing a part, as Frenchmen did, to get the attention and the admiration of the crowd. Rousseau saw the English as more solitary, more confident in themselves, less caring about others' opinions of them. They liked to think things out on their own, and the novel was designed to meet just such a taste. In one of his many striking phrases, Rousseau considered the English more concerned with being happy than giving the appearance of being happy. It was the drama which encouraged 'silly imitations'.

Diderot, a key influence on French 18th century thought, essentially agreed with Rousseau in his 'Praise of Richardson' (1760), praise from a leading French critic for an English novelist. Earlier he had already castigated drama for its dependence on 'ceaseless, feverish action'. Theatre was for those who surrendered to immediate pleasure and were essentially facile. The novel was for the calm, self-centred man who left behind the tiresome pleasures of the social round and retired to his own study for quiet reflection.

Madame de Staël's 'Literature and Social Institutions' (1800), claimed even more for the novel. Whereas in classical Greece political decisions were shared out among the citizens of the state, and the epic poem and the drama celebrated the public actions of committed citizens doing their bit for the group, in 1800 it was different. Political liberty depended on keeping a private place around oneself where the too powerful state could not interfere. Freedom meant being free from government intervention. This was a concept no ancient Greek would have understood. Madame de Stael, recognising this concept as the mainspring for so much English political thought, saw English writers as supreme exponents of the novel, because their fiction celebrated, 'morality in which minor qualities and fates create a new kind of heroism'.

These are only particularly illustrious examples of widely held views that underpinned Jane Austen's certainty in 1814. The drama was suspect, depending for its effects on what characters did, on their actions on stage. The novel looked at the inner processes of thought that preceded action, and could carefully weigh 'thoughts that do lie too deep for tears'.

Jane Austen's characters attend plays just as they attend 'balls' in London or in Bath, as part of the round of social activities that make up a morally question-able 'season'. What matters in the novels is what the characters think and feel rather than what they do, and this, it was felt, was an area where the drama could not compete. As Jane Austen makes clear in her eulogy of the novel in 'Northanger Abbey', the reader has direct access to the mind of the novelist. The poor playwright can only reach his audience through the actions of his invented characters. The novelist can speak directly to readers, sharing innermost thoughts with them as the story proceeds.

It is difficult for us now to realise just how damaging to the theatre these views, so trenchantly stated by so many critics and commentators, proved to be. They made the theatre seem an intellectually shoddy place. By the end of the 19th century Henry James (himself a failed playwright, although a successful novelist), could roundly state of the England he had adopted as his country, 'the arts of the stage are not really in the temperament and manners of the people. These people are too highly moral to be histrionic … they have too stern a sense of duty'. Morality once again. Although there is more than a hint of a bad workman blaming his tools, Henry James is complaining, at least in part, about puritan prejudice. What he is really saying is that the theatre is immoral, too scandalising for the high moral tone of the English people. It was in this climate that Oscar Wilde wrote 'An Ideal Husband', George Bernard Shaw his theatre criticism, and Archer tried to eulogise Ibsen. They were struggling against a tide of thought that had left theatre deserted by intellectuals for over two centuries. As Shaw's perceptive dustman in 'Pygmalion' reminds us, 'middle class morality' was undoubtedly the culprit, but where had that morality come from? A long line of so-called critics must be held responsible, with Rousseau and the French Encyclopaedists in the vanguard.

The 20th century saw the tide change. Film, radio and finally television immersed everybody in exactly the kinds of drama that Rousseau, Diderot and de Staël despised. A Schwarzenegger film has just the kind of 'ceaseless, feverish action' Diderot would abhor. By the end of the 20th century almost the whole world was back in the playhouses of these new media, wallowing in the illusions and pretences Rousseau was so anxious to save the solid burghers of Geneva from experiencing.

Was he right? Have we changed for the worse? Most of us would now agree that these critics quite simply got it hopelessly wrong. The idea that only in the novel can the writer address his audience directly is obviously unfair. One of the essential roles of the chorus in classical Greek drama was to comment on the action as it unfolded, to stand back and take a larger view. Would anyone suggest that Shakespeare in his soliloquies did not take the audience into the mind, the secret thoughts, the motives and the very psychology of his believable characters?

All Rousseau's strictures against unhealthy feelings, pretence and illusion, audiences losing themselves in the false emotions of others, fragmenting their own identity as in imagination they step into the shoes of invented characters and experience their imaginary thoughts in created situations – all these criticisms apply just as much to the novel as to the play. Any burghers in Geneva weeping over Samuel Richardson's 'Clarissa', 'Pamela' or 'The History of Sir Charles Grandison', were experiencing very similar emotions to an audience for Euripedes or Shakespeare. Accustomed as we now are to the film of the play of the book, we can see that Sir Thomas Bertram got it wrong. The theatre languished in the intellectual doldrums, and was looked down on for over two centuries, largely as the result of influential critics' mistaken and wrongheaded theories.

Growing Importance of Art Criticism

THE ELEMENT TO notice is that art critics were indeed influential. Their steady growth in status and the growing number of media from which they promulgated their views, must be seen against a wider background of cultural change, where the media of communication became increasingly important. At the same time, the role of criticism and the critic came under more and more scrutiny as part of an intellectual debate. Edmund Burke's 'A Philosophical Enquiry into the Origin of our Ideas of the Sublime and the Beautiful' (1757), is a fairly typical example. It was a subject much thought about. From Francis Hutcheson's 'An Inquiry into the Original of our Ideas of Beauty and Virtue' (1725) or David Hume's 'Of the Standard of Taste' (1757) or Lord Kames' 'Elements of Criticism' (1762) to William Hogarth's 'Analysis of Beauty' (1753), there were two main areas of debate. It was agreed that the response to beauty was individual and subjective, essentially a matter of feeling and emotion. Yet at the same time these thinkers were searching for rules that could be laid down, standards that could be generally agreed, about what was right and what was wrong in aesthetic judgements. They were looking for guidance in matters of taste. They wanted to equip the critic with the correct armoury to enable him to make the right judgements over what was beautiful and what was not. With hindsight there seems something deliciously illogical about the whole debate. How can a response which is emotional possibly be judged as being right or wrong? Yet the search was obstinately conducted. As Burke put it, the aim was:

> To find whether there are any principles, on which the imagination is affected, so common to all, so grounded and certain, as to supply the means of reasoning satisfactorily about them. And such principles of taste I fancy there are, however paradoxical they may seem to those who on a superficial view imagine that there is so great a diversity of tastes, both in kind and degree, that nothing can be more indeterminate.

It was not until Kant, as we shall see, that this problem was resolved to the satisfaction of philosophy. But before looking at that, however it is time to consider the next major development in European culture, labelled by historians 'Romanticism'.

Romanticism

HISTORIES OF THE 18th and 19th centuries make clear how the agricultural and industrial revolutions changed the Western world, changed the way people lived and, with increasing waves of new technology, accustomed everybody to an accelerating rate of what has since seemed almost ceaseless innovation. What is perhaps less recognised is the almost cataclysmic effect these changes had on popular culture. Nor is it fully appreciated that the world of the countryside, seemingly so impervious to change, was itself altered almost out of recognition, just as much as the newly industrialised cities. The result was a cultural watershed, after which nothing was ever going to seem the same again.

The population of England in the 1700s was little more than 5 million, yet by the 1850s this had grown to little less than 25 million. Judged by any previous standards this was a staggering increase that took place over little more than four generations. In terms simply of the buildings to house this astonishing increase, the communications and organisation required to feed and clothe them, the jobs necessary for the steadily expanding workforce, this was very much a real revolution.

The cosy world of the countryside was equally over-turned and in much the same time span. The old world where the majority of that 5 million lived in small villages, each household owning strips of land in three great fields which surrounded the village, each field lying fallow every third year in rotation, was largely swept away. Innovation and experiment brought in new farming methods. The enclosures that followed trans-formed rural society into a different world. The coun-tryside was now divided into aristocratic landowners, a minority of yeoman farmers owning their own land, a much greater number of farmers renting their land from landowners, and with every farm employing a new breed of landless labourer working for depressingly low wages.

Agriculture's increased efficiency meant that more food was produced with much less labour, so there were fewer jobs available, and a steady stream of unemployed workers drifted into the newly industrialised cities to be swallowed up in the new factory system organised around the new source of power, the steam engine. For the first time, mankind could have power when and where it was wanted, and a host of inventive machines appeared in lively response to the challenge. Workers in these factories toiled for long hours in grim conditions and lived in appallingly overcrowded slums where life was, as Hobbes had put it, indeed 'nasty, brutish and short'.

These cities were a new phenomenon. A workforce torn from a variety of backgrounds had to learn to live a new kind of social living, and the industrial cities had to learn themselves how to deal with a new set of social problems: sewage, sanitation, water supply, health, public safety, public order, and many more. A whole rural way of life was ruthlessly transformed in the new market economy and more and more of the steadily growing 25 million lived in the new cities rather than in the countryside at all. In the midst of all this upheaval, what chance was there that the old folk culture, which had slowly evolved around small village life and sleepy market towns, could survive? How could it compete against the sheer numbers living a different kind of life in a savagely transformed world?

Where the working class in the cities were being grimly exploited, a new class was growing in numbers, power and influence. The middle class, the small entrepreneurs, the inventive engineers, the expanding merchant fleet, the traders, the foremen in the factories, the lawyers, the doctors and the teachers were all keeping this industrialised world going and making it and themselves increasingly prosperous. They were building large, comfortable homes to live in and saving about half their annual income, savings which helped provide the capital to keep the system expanding.

Increasingly, from the beginning of the 18th century, the media, particularly the worlds of newspapers, pamphlets, and magazines like 'The Tatler' and 'The Spectator', addressed themselves to this rising middle class. It is instructive to compare the criticism of Dryden in the previous generation, with that of Joseph Addison (1672-1719) and Richard Steele (1672-1729) in 'The Spectator'. Dryden wrote his literary criticism as a fellow poet, playwright and writer, sharing the problems of authorship. He saw Shakespeare and Jonson, Horace or Juvenal as fellow craftsmen tackling the same problems as he did as a writer. The readers he addressed were essentially members of a small intellectual elite, well educated and equally learned as himself. He thought of himself as writing for equals who like him had already arrived at sound judgements. Addison, Steele and the outstanding critic of their generation, Dr Samuel Johnson (1709-84), were different. They saw themselves as helping to mould judgements in their readers, and patiently expounded reasons to convince them. This was more than a difference of tone. It was a recognition that a new class of readership had arrived on the scene anxious to learn, and learn not only about art, but about a whole range of social behaviour and political opinion. 18th century critics consciously saw themselves as helping to educate their readers. Sir Joshua Reynolds, founder and first president of the Royal Academy of Arts, in his influential 'Discourses' to the students of the Academy from its official opening in 1769 to his last in 1790, two years before his death, adopted much the same approach. His lectures were published and reached a much wider audience than the students of the Academy.

It was a rather different matter with the wives and daughters of the new middle class. Women who a generation or so earlier would have been peasants, probably working even harder than their men folk in the old village economy, now found themselves to be 'ladies' with plenty of servants to do the house work and no possibility of any career for themselves beyond getting married and adding to the expanding population. They had to find ways of passing the time, and came to represent the first mass consumer demand for the arts. Lending libraries, newspapers, magazines, novels, plays, even opera and ballet, all came to their rescue. The women in this middle class were not particularly well educated, but they had money to spend and the arts changed radically to meet this new demand.

The concepts of romantic love, sensationalism, sentimentality, escapism and a new humanitarian approach to politics, which included an abhorrence of slavery, were all part of these changes – changes which cultural historians have labelled 'Romanticism'. Attitudes, assumptions, almost an entire ideology, altered irrevocably. For example in the early 1700s young people expected their parents to arrange a marriage for them. By the 1800s this was already being questioned and by the 1900s, few young people would have sanctioned it.

Romanticism, as it became more influential from the end of the 18th century onwards, changed cultural attitudes and assumptions at a time when, as we have seen, social changes were altering the ways people lived and related to each other. Whereas in the heyday of the classical period, influential 18th century critics like Dr. Johnson, Addison and Steele had valued 'raison' and 'lumiere', welcoming a balance between warring emotions which had to be subordinated to the power of reason, Romanticism almost expected emotion to be pushed to excess. From William Beckford's 'Vathek' (1786) onwards, urged on by a new tribe of writers and critics, novels, plays, operas, ballets and fiction in magazines positively wallowed in the extremes of passion. This was the age of the 'horror' novel, of ghosts and horrid things that went bump in the night. In countless five volume novels and stirringly melodramatic plays, terrified maidens immured in turrets listened in growing hysteria as something loathsome clanked its slimy way up the stone spiral steps towards them. In the ballet 'Giselle' (1841), a whole act was devoted to ghosts making unfortunate young men dance to death! Rochesters had homicidal maniacs chained up in their attics and 'Dracula' was waiting impatiently to be born and immediately became a best-seller.

Yet Romanticism was much more than a 'dumbing down' of the arts in response to the first mass consumer demand from poorly educated middle class women with time on their hands. It was a major change in the attitudes and assumptions of critics, intellectuals and creative artists across the whole range of the fine arts. It encompassed a major shift in the status of the creative artist. This is best exemplified by comparing two generations of composers. Joseph Haydn (1732-1809), although a composer with an international reputation, spent most of his working life as a senior servant in the aristocratic family of the Esterhazys. He was in charge of the small orchestra that played for the family on social occasions. He ate with other senior servants in the servants' hall. His contract specified his hours, duties and even what he should wear. His pupil, Ludwig van Beethoven (1770-1827), also had contracts. They were with his publishers. He had an independent income from his music which enabled him to live and love in some style, and feel just as good as anybody else, including aristocrats. Romanticism brought together concepts that had been around in earlier periods, but only at the edge, on the periphery of people's thinking about the fine arts, and made these concepts central and significant. The artist was seen as a potential genius, whose inspiration came not as a result of being possessed by some heavenly force from above, but from within himself, from his own creative imagination, which, and this was of major importance, enabled him to be original in his artistic creations, to break new ground and establish fresh means of expressing his own personal vision, and thus manage to communicate through the symbolic language of his art, universally shared emotions and sentiments. Almost inevitably such a gifted creator was bound to be a rebel, no longer prepared to work within the traditional standards of his art. These were the attitudes of Romantic poets like Keats, Wordsworth, Shelley, Byron and Coleridge.

Shelley in particular was wonderfully vituperative about critics. In a few lines in 'Adonais', he manages to call them 'herded wolves', 'obscene ravens', 'vultures' and 'spoilers'. Of course he did not mean all critics, just those he disagreed with. After all, perhaps the most influential literary critic of his day was no less a person than Coleridge himself. Samuel Taylor Coleridge (1772-

1834), was co-author with Wordsworth of the 'Lyrical Ballads' which did much to get Romanticism established in English literature. In spite of the addiction to opium which in effect, ruined his life, he was not only an outstanding poet, but also a major and very influential critic He introduced the word 'aesthetic' to the English language, and in lectures, newspaper and magazine articles he spread the thinking of Immanuel Kant (1724-1804), whose philosophic work underpinned much of Romanticism. Kant thought that only a creative artist in the fine arts was to be considered a genius, what he called 'meisterhafte originalitat'. He considered that the aesthetic response was special and different from other emotional responses. Being different, it required its own special consideration.

Coleridge seems to have picked up many of Kant's ideas second hand from reading another German philosopher, Schelling, and by the time the British public got them from Coleridge third hand, they could be pretty impenetrable. There has, for example been much discussion about what Coleridge really meant in these often quoted sentences:

> The primary imagination I hold to be the
> living power and primary agent of all human
> perception, and as a repetition in the infinite
> mind of the eternal act of creation in the infinite

I AM. The secondary imagination I consider as an echo of the former, co-existent with the conscious will, yet still as identical with the primary in the kind of its agency, and differing only in degree and in the mode of operation.

This compares fairly well for impenetrability with the sentence quoted earlier from Hermogenes, and I doubt if even the most baffling of the French structuralists could do much better. Embedded in a great gush of Coleridge's conversation, it would probably sound impressive and would rush by unquestioned since, as Madame de Staël remarked, 'Avec Monsieur Coleridge, c'est toujours le monologue!'

The Influence of Ruskin

Even more important than Coleridge was the 19th century critic John Ruskin (1819-1900). He followed on behind Augustus Welby Pugin, a brilliant architect and powerful writer, whose masterpiece in partnership with Barry was the rebuilding of the Houses of Parliament in the new Gothic Revival style which he advocated. Ruskin was undoubtedly the major art critic of the Victorian period. He began by writing about painting, particularly J.M.W. Turner, and his very first book, 'Modern Painters' (1843) revealed an author of deep and sympathetic sensibility, who wrote marvellous prose. He continued to write astonishingly well about painting, and became a champion for the Pre-Raphaelites. After visiting Italy, and in particular Venice, he too fell in love with the Gothic style of architecture and with a Romantic vision of the medieval period to which it belonged, he wrote persuasively about it, and in memorable prose, dismissed the classical style in architecture out of hand. Together with Pugin, they became major influences in transforming Victorian taste in architecture. It has been said that

Pugin made English architecture Gothic and Ruskin made it Italian.

The school which I attended, Dulwich College, would not have its present form, had it not been for Pugin, Ruskin and Barry. It was built in 1866-70 by Barry's son Charles Barry Junior (1823-1900) and has a campanile identical to that of S.Maria della Carita in Venice, and is taken from a painting of 1728 by Canaletto, 'The Stonemason's Yard', which is in the National Gallery. That building collapsed in 1744, but Barry took his inspiration from the painting. He crammed the rest of his building with attractive ornaments from other Italian Gothic buildings, and the result is that, somewhat improbably, an Italianate palazzo, complete with Venetian campanile, sits a shade uncomfortably in the prim and proper London suburb of Dulwich. The poet and author, Lawrence Durrell (1912-90) said of it, 'A fair candidate for the wildest 19th century building in London, with a crazy Dostoevskian gleam in its eye'. I was there during World War II, when it was fashionable to sneer at all things Victorian, but my fellow pupils and I were secretly very fond of it. When a bomb destroyed the science block, which was ugly and had been added much later, we felt it was no more than it deserved, although admittedly when bombs fell on the hallowed ground of the First XI cricket pitch we all felt exposed to the brutality of the conflict, and that this was undoubtedly war with the gloves off!

I mention it because it is a good example of the ways in which Victorian architectural critics, particularly Pugin and Ruskin, broke down an almost universal dependence on the classical style, and opened the way to what became a Battle of the Styles. Towards the end of the century almost any style, from Indian to Moorish Spanish, was acceptable as the outer skin of a building, which then bore little relation to its structure. Gradually the Arts and Crafts movement, for which paradoxically Ruskin was himself originally responsible, brought back some kind of sanity. Most of us would regard the domestic architecture of C.F.A. Voysey (1857-1941) or the grander country houses of Edwin Lutyens (1869-1944) as among the high points of English architecture. Yet alas, once again a remarkably influential critic and historian, Nicholas Pevsner (1902-83), almost single-handedly changed the course of architectural development in this country. We are greatly indebted to Pevsner for his noble series 'The Buildings of England'. I myself worked with him on researching Victorian theatre architecture in the 1960s, and can testify to the breadth of his learning and perceptive approach to buildings. Yet Pevsner idolised the stark continental so-called functional or rectangular style of 'modern' architecture, exemplified by Le Corbusier (1887-1965) or Mies van der Rohe (1886-1969) and used his influence to ensure that its adherents were strategically placed in the education of the next generation of British architects. I know that C.F.A. Voysey was horrified when Pevsner hailed him as 'one of the pioneers of the modern movement.' Much of the dull or positively awful municipal architecture of the '60s, '70s and '80s can be laid firmly at Pevsner's door as a result of his influence.

In his writings on architecture Ruskin put much emphasis on 'truth of expression' in structure and materials. But since he was fascinated by ornament, and hotly opposed to machines as such, and to standardised construction, he can hardly be thought of as a pioneer of functionalism and so-called modern architecture. Later in his life he followed the lead of Thomas Carlyle in opposing the values of political economists, and spread a misty eyed picture of the advantages of the medieval world, which greatly influenced William Morris and many of the founders of the Labour Party. He is always a pleasure to read, and remains an example of a critic persuading by the sheer brilliance of his prose style.

Unfortunately for him, he became involved in a famous court case in 1878 whose repercussions on art criticism are still felt to this day. In 1877 Ruskin published in his journal 'Fors Clavigera' a review of paintings in the Grosvenor Gallery, which championed the new Aesthetic movement of 'Art for Art's sake'. (It was satirised in Gilbert and Sullivans's 'Patience' as 'greenery yallery, Grosvenor gallery'.) Ruskin praised Edward Burne-Jones, but then said of a 'Nocturne' by Whistler, 'I have seen and heard much of cockney impudence before now, but never expected to hear a coxcomb ask two hundred guineas for flinging a pot of paint in the public's face'. James Abbot McNeill Whistler (1834-1903) commenced an action for libel, and the court case became a 'cause celebre' in the media, attracting much public debate. It seemed a clear cut case of the old refusing to accept the new. Ruskin thought that the beauty found in nature and in the human form represented God's goodness, and an artist's job was to be true to this nature and so reveal God's goodness to his public. For an artist to be conceited enough to try and improve upon nature was immoral. Whistler thought an artist should only be concerned with his art and not be concerned with moral or propaganda effects on the society in which he painted. Ruskin's lawyer asked Whistler how long the painting took, and when told only a couple of days, commented, 'the labour of two days for which you are asking two hundred guineas!'

Whistler famously replied, 'No, I ask it for the knowledge I have gained in the work of a lifetime.'

Whistler had asked for a thousand pounds in damages. The jury, while granting that he had indeed been libelled, awarded him a mere farthing in damages. The crippling legal costs of the case meant that Whistler was made bankrupt and had to sell everything, including his Chelsea house. He spent almost all the next two years in Venice, and on his return to London, exhibited the pastels he had painted there. He commented, 'They are not as good as I supposed. They are selling!' In 1885 he published his first book, 'Ten O'Clock Lecture'. Oscar Wilde reviewed it as a 'masterpiece', 'not merely for its clever satire and amusing jests … but for the pure and perfect beauty of many of its passages … for that he is indeed one of the very greatest masters of painting, in my opinion. And I may add that in this opinion Mr. Whistler himself entirely concurs.'

The Aesthetic Movement or Art for Art's Sake, had arrived on the London art scene, with its Yellow Books, its Beardsley drawings, its wits exchanging epigrams, and its delicate flirtations with decadence. What had also arrived, largely as a result of the Whistler v. Ruskin trial, was a public debate about art and about criticism.

Art Critics' Loss of Confidence

Ruskin, with all the grandeur of his writings and status as the leading critic of his day, had lost, had failed to convince, had been shown in a court of law to have been wrong. The reputation, the moral authority of critics suffered a serious blow. And no one knew this better than the critics of the time. Their tone undoubtedly altered, they became less willing to offer judgements and more ready to try sympathetically to establish what the artist was attempting to achieve. Unfortunately for them, an even worse example was about to arrive, making the whole tribe of art critics seem even more mistaken than Ruskin had been. After all, with Ruskin it had been touch and go, with only a farthing in damages. With the French Impressionists, the public learned just how mistaken critics could be.

As far back as 1863, with the first Salon des Refusés in Paris, artists were able to exhibit work that had been rejected by the committee of the official Salon. A number of impressionist works in their new style were shown there, and attracted much public ridicule from the art critics. Louis Leroy, a leading art critic, fastened on the title of one painting, 'Impression: Sunrise', and used the word to cover a particular group of artists, led by Renoir, Monet, Sisley and Bazille, and the term caught on and its use became general. Whistler himself exhibited in the first Salon des Refusés. Art critics had a lot of fun with the Impressionists. It was suggested that pregnant women should not be allowed in the gallery, since the shock might prove too great. During the Franco–Prussian war it was even suggested that Impressionist paintings might be used to stop the advancing Germans dead in their tracks. In 1863 Napoleon III himself declared that Manet's 'Le Dejeuner sur L'Herbe' was an insult to modesty. Tradition has it that he was almost moved to strike it with his stick. We can all understand his feelings when faced with what we consider the incomprehensible masquerading as art. I myself felt something similar when faced with Tracey Emin's 'Unmade Bed'. Indeed when the publisher of this book, James Hogan, and myself visited Tate Modern on the first day it was open to the public, right at the top of the building we entered a room that was clearly not yet finished. Interior decorators' tools and paints were still strewn about. James Hogan decided to make a joke of it. "Now this is one of the finest pieces of conceptual art we have yet seen," he said. "The compelling force of the asymmetry, the sheer originality of it quite take my breath away!" A gallery attendant was not amused, and rebuked us. "It is supposed to be an exhibit and part of the show", he said reprovingly. We retreated in some disorder. It was the same for those French critics in 1863, because just as we have seen the public flocking into Tate Modern, so after nearly twenty years of ridicule from the art establishment, the Impressionist painters gradually became the darlings of the public, and have largely remained so ever since.

An even worse example arrived in 1913 at the Theatre des Champs Elysées in Paris, when the audience booed and jeered at Stravinsky's 'Rite of Spring' choreographed by Nijinsky. It took very little time for people to realise this was in fact a musical masterpiece, which has been much loved and appreciated ever since.

Art criticism has never fully recovered from these appalling failures on the part of the critics. With the awful example of their predecessors in mind, art critics, particularly those of painting and sculpture, became increasingly reluctant to express any kind of judgement on the artistic merit of what was on offer. Instead, meekly and tamely, they became more inclined to ask what the artist was attempting to achieve.

Modernism

VIRGINA WOOLF SOMEWHAT mischievously declared that, 'On or about December 1910, human character changed.' She was referring to that widespread sense that the 20th century was somehow 'modern' where previous centuries were not. The actual date of the change is arguable, but there is no doubt that in the fine arts, the distinction is clear enough. From about 1910 onwards, there has always been a feeling that it is somehow necessary to make allowances when approaching the arts of previous centuries. 'If only they had known what we know, felt what we feel, understood what we understand, they would have thought and acted differently.' However gifted, however creative those great artists of the past were, they cannot be expected to show the kind of sophistication we have a right to expect from artists today, because they existed in the strait-jacket of their own historical period, which inevitably cuts them off from our own. We experience life differently from earlier times, and the arts have changed to respond to that difference. Obviously a wide range of influences have gone into making the mindset which we regard as 'modern'. The weakening of religion, the theory of relativity, the awareness of the unconscious, the arrival of the mass media for a growing industrialised society: there are almost as many alleged causes as there are theorists about them. Most commentators would agree that the works of Darwin, Marx and Freud have all played a part in effecting the change to 'modernity'. No art critic worth his salt can afford to ignore them. Here we shall briefly attempt to summarise their contribution and their importance.

Did Darwin Destroy God?

ONE OF THE major influences in creating modern attitudes and assumptions was Darwin's 'On the Origin of Species' (1859). His theory came as a shattering revelation in its day. Darwin was a scientist, and science proceeds by carefully scrutinising whatever evidence is available, and then suggesting a hypothesis to explain the facts so scrutinised. The hypothesis can then be tested in further experiments, and if these support it, the hypothesis holds the field until someone comes up with a better explanation. The brilliance of Darwin's theory has been that all later tests, discoveries and evidence have only served to reinforce his original proposals. He suggested that all the various species around us had evolved from a single stem, that each species struggled to survive and evolve in a 'nature red in tooth and claw' as Tennyson would later put it, and that natural selection weeded out those less able to survive as their environment changed or other species elbowed them out. His theory has enabled us to look with fresh insight into the world of living things and paved the way for a whole array of discoveries including DNA. Although he never worked them out in any detail with reference to humankind, his theories had obvious implications for the role of humans in relation to other living things. Christianity baldly stated that God had created man, and then woman, and given them 'dominion' over the rest. As Darwin's theories sank into general consciousness, it became ever clearer that mankind was in fact nothing more than a superior ape, and a remarkably late arrival on the life of the planet earth, which had existed for billions of years longer than the Bible said it had. Darwin's theories were a major blow to the authority of the Bible, and to much Christian teaching, and in some areas of backward thinking, so-called 'creationists' are still trying to refute and deny the overwhelming evidence that now supports Darwin's proposals.

In Britain there has been in the twentieth and twenty first centuries, a remarkable fall in Church of England attendances, and in general, plenty of evidence that Christian religion does not mean as much to the average citizen as it clearly did in previous centuries. Darwin must obviously bear at least some of the blame (or credit?) for this. Did Darwin in fact destroy God?

To try and answer this question may I first speculate about Early Man, Cro-Magnon Man, our direct ancestor, the first appearance on the planet of men and women with all the attributes we now possess? No doubt my speculations will make a social anthropologist wince, but since we know so little about early man, my speculations are as essentially unprovable as anybody else's. Imagine early man in his cave, with thunder and lightning building up a storm outside. These natural phenomena must have been extraordinarily frightening. Yet if they could be explained in terms say, of the anger of the Great God Wuzz, who was angry with us because we had broken his rules, and if early man took his first-born daughter to the sacrificial stone at the mouth of the cave and slit her throat to placate the God's anger, what is really happening? The unknowable has become knowable. We now know what thunder and lightning are. The uncontrollable has become controllable. We can placate God's anger and the thunder and lightning will stop. Even more importantly, man becomes the centre of the universe since it is all happening because the Great God Wuzz is annoyed with us. It is a truism to point out that much of the force and appeal of early religions depend on this process, making the frightening world explicable, knowable, controllable and reassuring the individual by giving him or her a false sense of their own importance in the general scheme of things. Yet the disadvantages of such religions is that they explain the world in affirmations that demand blind faith and cannot be questioned. If the world is supported, let us say, on the shoulders of a giant, who is standing on a crocodile, supported by a turtle, to question this is blasphemy and such questionings have to be punished.

In Western culture, which we like to believe stems from the ancient Greeks, early Greek religion explained thunder and lightning in terms of an angry Father of the Gods, Jove, hurling thunderbolts. Yet alone among the peoples around them, the Greeks were prepared to speculate that the real reasons for thunder and lightning might be quite different. It is this willingness to speculate without any sense of blasphemy which made the Greeks special. They seem to have been the first people to believe there are rational answers to rational questions, when faced with the tangible phenomena which made up their world. Of course this belief that there are rational answers to rational questions is itself a paradox. There is nothing rational about belief. Yet the whole of Western science is based on this belief that there are rational answers to rational questions.

Partly the Greeks felt able to put these questions because their early religion was anthropomorphic. Whatever an ancient Greek wanted to do, make love, get drunk, work hard, fight well – there was a god or a goddess in favour of it. Feminists will note that there were goddesses as well as gods. There was not much sense of sin either, and no concept of hellfire waiting in the afterlife, just a dusty Hades for all our shadows after death, all the emphasis being on making the most of life here and now while it challengingly existed within our grasp, to be experienced and to be understood.

In the same tradition of science established by the Greeks, Darwin asked questions, based on the evidence available, and his theory and the subsequent discoveries of overwhelming evidence to support it, made it increasingly impossible to accept the Bible as a literal account of the world's creation. This made it possible to stand back and see that at least part of the appeal of Christianity was the same as that of all primitive religions: it made the unknowable, knowable; the uncontrollable, controllable; and put mankind firmly in the centre of the universe. In the twenty-first century, at least partly as a result of Darwin's proposals, we know enough to be sure that there is still a great deal we do not know, a great deal that we cannot hope to control, and that we are very far from being the centre of the universe.

Does this mean that Darwin destroyed God? The evidence would seem to suggest not.

Perhaps the first thing to note is the extraordinary resilience of religion. The Christian Church managed to survive Galileo's observations that directly disproved the Church's cosmology. A hundred years after Darwin, the Church is still resolutely trundling on. Nor is it necessary to maintain that Galileo or Darwin got it wrong. While no longer prepared to accept the primitive religious appeal of Christianity, there is an area of human experience that can best be described as spiritual, a sense of something other, an apprehension of what we call divine. A religion can be seen as a culture's attempt to come to terms with this area of human experience. Just as Arab culture produced the Muslim religion, Indian culture produced Hinduism, European culture produced Christianity. Each is relevant and bound up within its own culture's history, as a valid way of dealing with the spiritual experiences that human beings undoubtedly have.

I used to own (before a student stole it), a charming Victorian guide to Protestant Christianity, in the form of a dialogue between a governess and a pupil who asked awkward questions. One of the questions asked why if God was benevolent and good, he allowed terrible disasters like earthquakes and volcanoes. The governess' answer was very revealing. She suggested that if the pupil looked more closely at the geographical map she would see that the great majority of these disasters were confined to Roman Catholic countries! It is just this strident partisanship that the post-Darwin world should be learning to do without. (Only Plymouth Brethren will be allowed through the pearly gates. The rest of us are condemned to hellfire!) Once a particular religion is seen as one culture's historical attempt to deal with human spiritual experience, then each religion is as worthy of respect and acceptance within its own culture as any other. A Muslim's view of the world through the teachings of his religion is as valid and as worthy of respect as a Christian's. While fully accepting Darwin's theory in all its implications, I myself am still proud to be a Christian and a baptised and confirmed member of the Church of England. In spite of some of the appalling excesses of my Church's history, it is inextricably bound up with my sense of my own identity within my own culture. It also chimes in with undoubted spiritual emotional experience that cannot be denied. I am not solving intellectual problems by a denial of the supremacy of the intellect, but simply recognising that there is a small but important area of human experience, the spiritual, with which the intellect cannot cope adequately. 'There is more in heaven and earth than can be found in your philosophy, Richard Dawkins!'

Karl Marx and Art

A NOTHER THINKER EMBEDDED in the nineteenth century who became a major influence in the twentieth, was Karl Marx (1818-1883). He too, as we shall see, had cutting things to say about religion, but the main thrust of his theories lay elsewhere. It is difficult even to pin him down as a thinker. Was he a philosopher, a political economist, a historian, a political theorist, a sociologist, a communist or a radical revolutionary? There is a case to be made out that he was all of these. He certainly looked at the growth of society in a fresh way. 'The history of all hitherto existing society is the history of class struggle'. Looking at the history of Europe, he considered that just as capitalism had replaced feudalism, capitalism contained within it the seeds of its own decay and in time would inevitably be succeeded by socialism, which would again in time lead to a stateless, classless society that he designated pure communism. There would inevitably be a transitional period which he called 'the dictatorship of the proletariat'. Society could be analysed in terms of where economic power lay, and that power lay with whichever class controlled the means of production, distribution and exchange.

'The development of modern industry, therefore, cuts from under its feet the very foundations on which the bourgeoisie produces and appropriates products. What the bourgeoisie therefore produces, above all, are its own grave-diggers. Its fall and the victory of the proletariat are equally inevitable.' At the same time he argued that socio-economic change would be precipitated by international, revolutionary action.

The Bolshevik Revolution in 1917, with Lenin actively preaching his form of Marxism, gave Marx an awesome prominence in the rest of the Western world. By the end of the 20th century, there were not many places on the planet that had not been affected by Marx's theories. Many, including China, still are.

What was most valuable about his thinking were the ways in which he approached and analysed the history of society in economic terms. Before Marx, the economic elements in both history and any analysis of social growth had tended to be underrated. Marx redressed this balance. His emphasis on the class struggle as a main engine for social change and growth was also new and added a fresh dimension to any understanding of social development. Yet his economics have not withstood the test of time very well. John Maynard Keynes considered Marxism 'an illogical doctrine' and 'Das Kapital' (Marx's main economic treatise) as 'an obsolete textbook which I know to be not only scientifically erroneous but without interest or application for the modern world.'

Marx was trenchant about religion. He regarded ideology as the set of ideas, attitudes and assumptions which are dominant at any particular time in social growth. These ideas may be accepted by the overwhelming majority, but in fact they favour the interests of whichever class happens to be dominant and controls the means of production. The satirist and critic, Jonathan Swift, has two prisoners in gaol congratulating each other on belonging to a free country. In fact they are not free. They are in prison. But they cling to a maxim they know to be true, in the face of all the evidence to the contrary: 'It's a free country, isn't it?'

Marx said of religion, 'Religious suffering is, at one and the same time, the expression of real suffering and a protest against real suffering. Religion is the sigh of the oppressed creature, the heart of a heartless world, and the soul of soulless conditions. It is the opium of the people.' He regarded religion as one of the most powerful means by which the dominant class controlled the majority in the selfish interests of the dominant class. There was a particular irony to this, since in many ways Marxist communism as it developed, had all too many aspects of the religion it decried and wished to supplant.

It demanded a 'total' act of faith in Marxist analysis. A Marxist could understand and explain all social developments. This included the 'inevitability' of the collapse of capitalism, which the good Marxist was only hastening by active intervention. (Karl Popper considered this assumption that society develops according to fixed and identifiable rules as one of the worst and most dangerous aspects of 'historicism'.) There was also the final end of social development in a classless, communist utopia, dangerously similar to the paradise that awaits the good in the afterlife of most religions. It could be argued that the good Marxist in mid-twentieth century was merely exchanging one religion for another!

The Achilles heel of Marxism has always tended to be its inability to deal comprehensively with the arts. Art was seen and almost dismissed as propaganda for the brave new world of communism that was ultimately on its way. Marx never came to grips with what artists actually feel and create. In 'Das Kapital' he wrote:

> A spider conducts operations that resemble those of a weaver, and a bee puts to shame many an architect in the construction of her cells. But what distinguishes the worst architect from the best of bees is this, that the architect raises his structure in imagination before he erects it in reality.

This was as near as Marx came to dealing with the creative impulse of the artist. He did ask why ancient Greek art should retain an 'eternal charm' long after the social conditions that produced it had vanished into the past. He never suggested that since Greek art dealt with human nature, it might still have some relevance even in the changed social conditions of the present. He noticed perceptively, that popular narratives tended to reinforce the ideology of the dominant class. If economic power resided with the kings, then stories tended to be about kings and princes and princesses. If power moved to the aristocracy, then the stories tended to be about aristocrats. When power shifted to the bourgeoisie, then so did the stories. Today, he would have been pleased to observe the social power shifts involved in television programmes like 'Coronation Street' and 'EastEnders'.

Fortunately for Marx, a group of Marxist thinkers established the Institute for Social Research in Germany. They are known as the Frankfurt School and among those who have greatly refined his aesthetic theories, are Theodor Adorno, Erich Fromm, Max Horkheimer and Herbert Marcuse. Collectively their theories are grouped under the grand title of Critical Theory. Adorno in his 'Aesthetic Theory' (1970) established the idea of autonomous art and instrumentalist art, which has proved remarkably influential. Basically he regarded modern society as having been hopelessly 'corrupted' to such an extent that capitalist assumptions of profit and loss had invaded all areas of life, including the arts. He considered that 'instrumental' art both reflected and reinforced the dominant ideology of a capitalist society. It just so happened that I was reading Adorno's work when it first appeared, while I was on a very successful tour of China with the Royal Ballet. Since I was married to their leading ballerina, I had gone along for the ride. Rather surprisingly I found myself sitting at the top table in the Great Hall of the Peoples' Republic in Peking, attending a banquet given by the Chinese government to the company. For reasons I have still not fathomed, I was placed next to the Chinese Prime Minister, with of course an interpreter provided. To make conversation, I remarked on the Peking traffic. In those days this consisted mainly of large lorries and hordes of cyclists. None of the cyclists carried lights on their bicycles. The previous day I had witnessed a distressing accident, and I suggested that if cyclists carried lights, this could have been avoided. He clearly thought I was incredibly naïve, and carefully explained to me that my suggestion would involve setting up a factory to make batteries and another to make torches, all at considerable expense, and for what purpose? Merely to save a few lives that were far better sacrificed for the public good. It struck me that here, although admittedly in a communist country, was a good example of Adorno's 'instrumental rationalism', a specific form of rationality focusing on the most efficient or cost-effective means to achieve a specific end, but not in itself reflecting on the value of that end. The previous day I had watched someone dying in terrible pain on the street. I could not agree with the Prime Minister.

Adorno regarded autonomous art as the moment when an artist shook himself or herself free from the corrupting influence of capitalist society, and created something which while it might refer to, or represent or repudiate some aspect of its own art, had nothing to do with the value system or the social conditions of the society in which it was created.

In the same way those viewing or hearing the work of art had to shake themselves free of their social conditioning, and approach the work with open minds, and try to appreciate it entirely for what it had to offer as a work of art in its own right.

Paintings by William Blake, Samuel Palmer or Joseph Mallord William Turner are obvious examples of autonomous art. Paintings by George Morland, with their fresh faced, well-fed and prettily clothed peasants in sentimental situations, so clearly aimed at richer purchasers who wanted to feel that all was well with the actual agricultural world, are just as obviously what Adorno would regard as 'instrumental' paintings, corrupted by the capitalist society for which they were produced.

Yet in spite of the best efforts of the Frankfurt School, Marx gradually fell from favour in the 1980s and 1990s. Partly this was the result of the collapse of the USSR in the late 1980s, partly it was the result of new currents of political thought – feminism, gay rights, ecology, global warming and ethnic movements – but it was also because over-arching, grand theories which attempted to explain everything had come to seem pretentious and too simplistic. Modernism was giving way to post-modernism, a development which we shall examine later.

Freud and Art

A NOTHER MAJOR INFLUENCE on modern attitudes and assumptions has been Sigmund Freud (1856-1939). With the passing of the years, his reputation within psycho-analysis, a medical science which he practically invented, has suffered, particularly in his analysis of women. Yet there can be no doubt of his overwhelming influence on the ways we think about ourselves, and on our perceptions of the behaviour and identity of others. His suggestion that the human personality can be seen as a combination of the Ego, the thinking mind, the Superego, that part of the mind which tells us what is right and wrong, and the Id which represents the basic human urges, may not seem a particularly revolutionary set of categories. Where he was extraordinarily influential was in his suggestion that sex was the primary motivational energy for human behaviour. It is difficult to realise now, how disregarded sex had been in most dissertations on human personality and behaviour, before Freud. It was seen as one among many human appetites, but not as having much particular importance. Freud elevated it to the primary urge which motivates most human behaviour. He is directly responsible for the importance it is now accorded in any discussions of human relationships.

Even more important, perhaps, was his concept of the conscious mind, and the subconscious or unconscious. He suggested that we are consciously aware of only part of the workings of our own minds. We have a part of the mind, the subconscious, which works away without our being aware of what it is doing. He suggested that when we suffered what he called a trauma, a wounding experience, if it was too much for us to cope or deal with, we suppressed all memory of it in our conscious mind, and in a process he called repression, we consigned it to the subconscious. When running through an outline with students of Freud's achievements, at this point they tended to become restive and unwilling to accept the validity of what he was proposing. I would therefore point out that we had all gone through an extremely traumatising event of which we had no conscious memory whatever – the process of being born. There we were and had been for nine months, as babies in the womb, cosseted and cared for, with life support systems functioning just to keep us comfortable and happy, when suddenly, with no apparent warning, a whole sequence of appalling events ejected us into the outside world, where unknown, unfamiliar and demanding hands were slapping us and trying to make us breathe in air. Yet we have absolutely no memory of this painful and shocking sequence of events. Freud would suggest that we found it too traumatising to cope with and so suppressed all conscious memory, pushing the whole sequence down into our subconscious mind. Yet in Freud's view the subconscious was not a mere repository for painful experiences we could not cope with. All of them seethed away in the subconscious, trying to get back into the conscious mind, which would only allow them back if they were sufficiently disguised for the conscious mind not to realise what they really represented. As a result, symbols, certain shapes, certain colours, certain objects, even in some cases living things, became loaded with emotional significance for the individual, simply because they related to a trauma which had originally been suppressed and pushed down into the subconscious, and could only return if sufficiently disguised. Phallic symbols, representing the disguised male sexual organ, are a fairly typical example of this. Women who have a phobia, an unnatural fear of snakes, for example, can be explained in these Freudian terms. The snake has become a phallic symbol.

Dreams were also important for Freud as a key to what was going on in the subconscious. We can all remember having a nightmare, and waking up with obvious physical symptoms, crying tears perhaps, or covered in sweat, with an accelerated heartbeat, making it clear that we have been through an emotional experience. Sometimes we can even remember some of what the nightmare was about, and it seems so silly. Why on earth were we so upset about something so seemingly trivial. Freud would suggest that only if the subject matter is sufficiently disguised, can it surface in the conscious mind, and a trained psychoanalyst might well be able to interpret what these disguised events really embody, and they probably refer back to a repressed trauma.

Freud also believed that the early years of infancy were not only crucial to emotional and personality development, but were themselves too traumatising for us to remember consciously much about them. For Freud, the male baby was hooked into a possessive and erotic relationship with its mother, who became the source of pleasure, and the father, tending to take the mother's attention away from the baby, became a hated rival for her affections. Yet the father appeared to love the baby himself, wanted to play with it, tickle it, say loving things like 'Ootchy Coo' to it, and be generally proud and delighted with it. The baby has to cope with a hated rival who appears to love it, and the resulting tensions become too much and the whole set of conflicting emotions are consigned to the subconscious. This moment of repression is of central importance to

Freud. He describes it as the 'Oedipus Complex'. The male baby has lusted after its mother, wanting to achieve some sort of sexual union. As it becomes more and more aware of the father, it recognises the impossibility of rivalry, has hidden fears that the father may castrate it, and represses its incestuous desires, makes peace with the father and identifies with him, entering into the symbolic role of manhood. As a result we remember very little of our first years. On one thing Freud is very clear. The idea that until puberty we are childishly innocent of sex is a mistaken one. Sexual urges are manifest from birth, moving from the mouth as a first erogenous zone, to the anus and the faeces, which can be withheld or not, and then in time to the genitals proper.

There is another tension around the human condition. Freud saw us as wanting to enjoy ourselves, impelled to what he called the 'pleasure principle'. Unfortunately we have to work to live, what Freud called the 'reality principle'. We have to repress the urge to lie back and enjoy ourselves and submit to the harsh facts that we need to work to live. The hunter has to hunt. The gatherer has to gather. In the industrial world we need a wage or a salary. Bills have to be paid. For much of the time pleasure is deferred, and we repress the pleasure principle and accept the reality principle. Yet this repression, carried to extremes, can make us ill, can turn into neurosis. It has even been suggested that humans could be called the 'neurotic' animal, that we carry around with us, seething away in our subconscious, too many repressions. One outlet, one escape route from desires we cannot hope to satisfy, is the process Freud called sublimation. By immersing ourselves in creative activities like painting pictures, writing novels or poems, building cathedrals, railway stations or airports, in other words the whole range of activities encompassed within the word 'culture', we can temporarily escape the neurotic condition. This in Freud's view is the engine that powers the world of the arts, including their well known parasite, the arts critic! Just as the beds of flowers so admired in our gardens are really plants putting on an obscene sexual display (exposing themselves in public?), so the pictures on view in the National Gallery really represent their painters' attempts to sublimate and escape from the guilty desires their conscious minds have been busily repressing all their lives!

Gombrich has given us a fascinating analysis of Freud's own attitudes to art, and particularly painting, in a perceptive essay in his 'Reflections on the History of Art'. Basing his remarks on the evidence of Freud's letters (published in 1960), he points out that Freud reflected the typical views of well-educated Austrians of his day, and tended as a result of his education, to see paintings through the eyes of Goethe and Schopenhauer, in other words to look for their spiritual or emotional qualities, rather than their formal, technical or stylistic aspects. Gombrich also enjoys the pleasant irony, that although it was Freud's very theories of the unconscious that inspired and underpinned the Surrealist movement in art, Freud himself regarded the Surrealist painters as near lunatics and had no sympathy at all for their products! Freud himself dragged Leonardo da Vinci on to his psychiatrists couch, when subjecting his painting 'St Anne' to a detailed analysis, suggesting it revealed much about Leonardo's early childhood. To be fair to Freud, in his letters he did reveal that this was done in a playful mood and was not to be taken too seriously!

Ernst Kris in his 'Psycho-Analytic Explorations in Art' (1953), considers that it was in his theory of the origins of humour that Freud came closest to a theory of creativity in art. Freud was particularly concerned with the pun, the play on words, which since Shakespeare has tended to dominate English humour. Freud regarded playing with words as an early attempt to grapple with and master the use of language. As we grow up, it is something we all like to do. He also thought it one of the ways in which repressed ideas could escape from the unconscious provided they were sufficiently disguised and kept in check by the grammatical forms of the language used. The pun worked at least partly by hinting at things that were not spelt out. Oscar Wilde's well known reply to his hostess' query, 'Pray tell us Mr. Wilde, what is the essential difference between man and woman?', 'Madam, I cannot conceive!', or Hilaire Belloc's verse, 'When I am dead, I hope it may be said, His sins were scarlet; but his books were read', both hint at a great deal more than is actually said, and at least part of their appeal lies in what is unsaid. They are both skirting perilously over forbidden territory. The poet as well as the punster is restrained within the limits of the form they are using. The poet often needs to rhyme to be effective. Keats changed 'grief' to 'sorrow' simply in order to rhyme with 'to-morrow', in his 'Ode to a Nightingale'. Freud felt the painter too should be restrained by the sensible limits of his medium, hence his dislike of the all too graphic imagery of the Surrealists.

While we do not have to accept the full range of Freud's theories, much less the tortuously argued extensions of them asserted by the French structuralist, Lacan, it should be clear that these theories have already changed the way we think about ourselves and our relations with other people, particularly our close relations. The world of commercial advertising has fallen and fastened upon his theories about symbols, and convinced themselves they work effectively. Painters, sculptors and creators across the whole range of the arts absorbed his theories about symbolism, and they added a fresh dimension to a whole range of art works. Techniques found effective in commercial television and film adverts seeped into film makers vocabulary. That excellent film director, Ridley Scott began his career making advertising commercials. Many of Freud's concepts and quite a few of his technical terms have entered into ordinary, everyday language and thinking. There is no going back. Our post-Freudian world is a very different place from the curious innocence of the Victorian and even Edwardian world that preceded him. We have only to think of Lewis Carroll's obsession with the charms of little prepubescent girls, to realise how popular attitudes have changed. What the Victorians found charming, we would find rather sinister or at least, unhealthy.

Art, Structuralism and the 1960s

I STILL CONSIDER MYSELF extraordinarily lucky to have been in my thirties during the 1960s, young enough to enjoy this heady period of experiment and change in the arts, and yet just mature enough to be able to stand back and take a longer view. Throughout those exciting years I was an arts critic on a national broadsheet, 'The Sunday Telegraph', as well as being a full-time lecturer on university courses. I can even claim to have been the first to submit a proposal for a degree course in media studies to the Council for National Academic Awards, but since there was at that time no board to consider this, it was firmly rejected by the History board, the English Literature board and, not altogether predictably, by the Psychology board!

Looking at the wide variety of 'media studies' courses that have proliferated since then, and the hordes of eager students doing them, there must be many academics who wish those early blanket rejections had been more firmly adhered to.

As the head of a small academic department, it was during these years that I first became aware, like so many of my colleagues, of the new wave of theories about criticism in the arts and particularly literature, that was sweeping like an irresistible tide through the world of academic study. I had been brought up since my school-days on the so-called New Criticism of Eliot, Richards and Empson, but this new wave of critical theory was much newer than that. It started in the linguistics of Saussure added to the ideas of the Russian Formalists of the Russian Revolution, refined by the Prague School of linguistics in the 1930s and kept alive during the '40s and '50s in America by academics fleeing World War II in Europe. Their theories about language, art and sign systems in general were the methodological basis for a positive torrent of revolutionary research in the '60s, '70s and '80s that went under the general heading of Structuralism. With its base in Paris, with scholars like Levi-Strauss, Foucault, Lacan, Derrida, Althusser and Roland Barthes, the movement spread elsewhere on the Continent, with Russian semiologists taking a fresh look at the Russian formalists. It became steadily more and more influential in British university litera-ture, language and arts departments.

In the 1960s it was almost inextricably bound up with the radical political and revolutionary fervour of those now distant years. I remember being informed then by one of my lecturing staff, that although there would be nothing personal about it, and it would on the whole be done with regret, when the inevitable social and political revolution arrived, he would have no qualms about stringing me up from the nearest lamp post because I was too tainted with bourgeois, humanist liberalism to be allowed to survive in the new socialist paradise that was just around the corner. Obviously my neck has proved rather less vulnerable than he thought, but at the time he genuinely believed in the accuracy of what he was prophesying. It almost went without saying that he was as excited about structuralism as he was about my imminent demise in the coming political upheaval.

At the time, I was eking out the far from generous salary of an academic with additional dollops of cash from my regular stint as a weekly critic on 'The Sunday Telegraph', occasional appearances on radio and television arts programmes, and reviews in other more or less elitist arts periodicals. As the 1960s progressed into the 1970s and then the 1980s, it became increasingly clear that not just a gap, but a chasm was opening up between the language of arts criticism in the university world and the language of arts critics in the media. Already I was struggling with works like Erich Kahler's 'The Disintegration of Form in the Arts', James Johnson Sweeney's 'Vision and Image' or Morse Peckham's 'Man's Rage for Chaos: Biology, Behaviour and the Arts'. Works like these functioned at levels outside structuralism altogether, but as structuralism took hold, the academic world was increasingly using terms, theories, and assumptions that amounted to a new kind of jargon that the general public, and the critics who addressed the general public, found steadily more incomprehensible. Far from there being a fruitful interchange, there grew up disdain from the academic world and fear and loathing on the part of the media, that set the two sides increasingly apart.

There had been initially some opposition to structuralism in university departments, but there it became a battle, if battle there was, between old fogeys and new brooms, and time eventually cleared out most of the old fogeys. It should be appreciated how slowly the worlds of academe adjust to changes of any kind. When I went up to Oxford after the Second World War, I was taught by dons who had been in their prime during the 1930s, and been seduced by the then fashionable beliefs in communism and pacifism. Many of them clung fervently to their already outdated ideologies in spite of the irrefutable evidence that the world was changing around them. Eager young converts to structuralism in the late 1980s are no doubt still dominating their academic worlds today, and still instructing young students accordingly. Time has not dealt kindly with some of the key thinkers they then admired. Foucault died of AIDS, Roland

Barthes was killed in an unlikely collision with a milk float. Althusser murdered his wife and committed suicide. The Oxford Professor Terry Eagleton, whose classic 'Literary Theory' 'served as a goad and a guide' to structuralism when it first appeared in 1982, in the revised edition published in 1996, states baldly 'structuralism has already more or less vanished into the literary museum'.

What is it about structuralism that makes it so attractive to the academic mind? Partly because it has a range of scientific terms, and develops its own academic jargon, it helps to bolster the self confidence of academics studying the arts that they are as good as, if not better than, their colleagues in other disciplines. It could be seen as the arts lecturers' equivalent for the second law of thermodynamics, which C.P. Snow made so much of. Partly too, it provides an immediate answer to the kind of jibes that those propounding aesthetic theories invariably find themselves facing. David Lodge in a perceptive essay in his 'Working with Structuralism', quotes from D.H. Lawrence's 1928 essay on John Galsworthy as a typical example of this antagonism.

> Literary criticism can be no more than a reasoned account of the feeling produced upon the critic by the book he is criticising. Criticism can never be a science: it is in the first place

much too personal, and in the second, it is concerned with values that science ignores. The touchstone is emotion, not reason. We judge a work of art by its effect on our sincere and vital emotion, and nothing else. All the critical twiddle-twaddle about style and form, all this pseudo-scientific classifying and analysing of books in an imitation-botanical fashion, is mere impertinence and mostly dull jargon.

Lodge rightly points out that Lawrence gives his own case away, by his use of the adjective 'reasoned'. If the critic's account is going to be 'reasoned', that presupposes some kind of analysis, some kind of classification. It is also significant that this quite heated diatribe against criticism, opens an informed and penetrating essay criticising Galsworthy!

Saussure, rightly seen as one of the founders of structuralism, severed the relationship between the word and the object it stands for. 'Egg' is a word, or a set of sounds uttered in speech, which produces in our minds the concept of that ovoid object hopefully found in a hen's nest. Saussure points out that the relationship is purely an arbitrary one. We say 'bacon and egg', but our language might just as well have developed so that we say 'bacon and ugg'. We simply happen to have settled in English for 'egg' rather than 'ugg'. Words have meanings in relationship to other words, not in relationship to things. Language is in effect a set of signs, making sense in relationship to other signs. Saussure called the word the 'signifier', and the concept which it evokes, the 'signified', and considered that any relationship between the signifier and the signified is an illusion. The word 'egg' is not an egg, it is an arbitrary sign for the concept of an egg, and has meaning in relation to other signs, which can be studied as a sign language, without any attempts to make omelettes or scrambled eggs.

Viewed in this way, language can be seen as a model for other sets of signs used in other arts, painting or sculpture say, or fashion or photography, which can all be studied in terms of their sign systems. This implies a revolutionary way of looking at the arts, of looking at form rather than content, of looking at the signifiers rather than the signified. Some structural theorists have taken this much further. What matters to them are the various ways the viewer or the reader interprets the signifiers, meaning that the signified, the actual content to which the signifiers refer, counts for less and less. It might be Shakespeare or it might be the 'Sun' newspaper, it hardly seems to matter since both can seemingly bear the full weight of structuralist jargon and analysis equally well.

This has wider implications. Since Aristotle, we have been brought up to think of art as 'mimesis', as an imitation of life. If we think of art as essentially a set of sign systems, making sense mainly in relation to other sign systems, then we can begin to sympathise with a view of art for art's sake. Art can be seen as existing in relationship with other arts and with what other artists have achieved in the past, rather than as an imitation of life. Oscar Wilde summarised this view in his challenging 'Life imitates Art', suggesting that the arts so manipulate and condition us that we perceive nature and life in the ways the arts have taught us to see and perceive them. This is a striking way of looking at culture generally. Art does not come from life, it comes from other arts and what earlier artists have already achieved. A painter facing his canvas depicts upon it what he has already learnt from other painters, or what he is reacting against in them. If he is facing a landscape, it is the way he depict it that matters, not the landscape itself. And what the painter paints will in turn condition the way we as viewers perceive both the painting and the landscape it supposedly depicts. We can begin to grasp what Pater meant when he wrote, 'All art aspires to the condition of music'. In music there is a sign language, sets of signs to be studied, but what is signified? It could be said that there is form, but to what external reality does it refer?

Plato it will be remembered was suspicious of music since it aroused undifferentiated emotion without directing it towards any set of goals. It was all form and no content.

Sentimentalists like to imagine that music is a universal language, speaking immediately to everybody, but a moment's reflection reminds us that this is not the case. Arab music, Chinese music, Indian music or African music are generally quite beyond the European music lover's taste and even understanding, and vice versa. Pater's dictum applies to the other arts busily aspiring to the condition of music. Arab, Chinese, Indian or African art tend to be equally beyond our ken, and are certainly each vigorously different from each other and from the European art tradition. If in each tradition artists have developed referring to what other artists within the tradition have already done, this certainly provides a Darwinian explanation for why each tradition has gone its own way and developed so differently from other traditions. It should be remembered too that each tradition has been underpinned by a different religion, providing different emphases and assumptions, so that it is not really surprising that a European painter, faced with a seascape should produce something so very different from what, say, Hokusai from within the Japanese tradition, might produce when faced with the same seascape. And if we accept Wilde's 'Life imitates Art', or Malraux's 'Art is born from Art', then it is presumably safe to assume that the average European 'sees' a slightly different seascape from the one the Japanese 'sees'. Each has been conditioned by their culture to 'see' the natural world slightly differently.

Art and Historicism

T HERE IS AN alternative view. This views the arts as unique human achievements which can only be fully understood when set in a historical context and interpreted as part of a historical process. One of the difficulties of this view is that a historian deals with facts. The Battle of Bosworth happened. Richard III was killed and Henry VII emerged as king and victor. The fact can be explained and interpreted in different ways, a Marxist historian would give a different account from a liberal humanist, but the facts remain facts, firmly set in the past. The arts are not like that. A landscape by Samuel Palmer is certainly a palpable fact. It was painted in a given year. But it comes alive again as a new experience every time a viewer sees it for the first time. In every audience for a performance of 'Hamlet' there will be those who have never seen the play before, and never even read it. They are responding to something fresh and new.

We must also beware of the dangers of what Karl Popper calls 'historicism', in his 'The Poverty of Historicism'. This is, 'an approach to the social sciences which assumes that historical prediction is their principal aim, and which assumes that this aim is attainable by discovering the 'rhythms', the 'patterns', the 'laws' or the 'trends' that underlie the evolution of history.' As Popper points out, this involves the concept of 'period'. 'Historicism claims that nothing is of greater moment than the emergence of a really new period', and that 'the only universally valid laws of society must be … the laws of historical development which determine the transition from one period to another.' Popper considers that this invests changes with the inevitability of the historical process and this gives them a dangerous kind of authority. It becomes necessary to adjust values and assumptions to fit in with the inevitable changes that a new period involves, and in the area of politics, which is Popper's main preoccupation, this can lead to varieties of totalitarianism. Sir Thomas More, executed on the scaffold for refusing to adjust to a new 'period' centuries before having the chance to read Popper, would doubtless have agreed with him given the chance. Popper specifically refers to 'aesthetic modernism or futurism', so we too must beware of losing our head over the inevitability of artistic changes.

Yet it is possible to view the arts, not as a hermetically sealed world within which artists have and are operating, but as one in which artists are constantly interacting with real life. The artist is constantly saying, 'Have you noticed this?' or 'Have you ever asked yourself why people do such and such?' or 'Just listen to this! I bet it will surprise you.' While there is no inevitability about the changes of fashion and style, they can be charted in relation to other historical changes taking place at the same time with which they interact, and on which they have some influence. It should be possible too, that like most of Wilde's challenging paradoxes, there is an element of truth in his 'Life imitates Art', but it does not describe the whole picture. Yes of course art conditions us to view the world in ways we have been taught, but the world is still out there, still challenging us to grapple with its problems and fascinating events. Darwin looking at finches on the Galapagos Islands did not see them as Landseer might have seen them, he saw evolutionary changes as a response to changing environments.

Modernism and Post-Modernism

Having accepted that Darwin, Marx and Freud, together with the structuralists, have conditioned us to view the world in ways which can be considered 'Modern', we should note in passing that this already seems out of date. 'Post-Modernism', the movement in all the fine arts which succeeded modernism, enables us with hindsight to take a measured view of what made modernism different. We can even venture on a few generalisations. Modernism as a movement, particularly in the period between World War I and World War II, seemed to become obsessed with form and technique as opposed to content and narrative. In the visual arts, representation gave way to increasing abstraction. Developments in the fine arts in the 20th century, initiated a growing divide between the fine arts and the general public. For almost the first time in cultural history, what leading artists were doing lost the respect, much less the appreciation and understanding, of the public at large. Modernism in music, for example, with the arrival of atonality, Schoenberg's twelve tone technique, polytonality, tone clusters, dissonant counterpoint and serialism, tended to produce baffled incomprehension even on the part of the regular concert going audience, itself very much a minority of the public for music. In architecture the general public tended to dislike the Bauhaus influenced buildings the architectural elite awarded each other prizes for. In painting and sculpture, cubism, surrealism, expressionism, futurism, and all the other 'isms' that came and went, seemed to move art works further and further away from what the public liked and enjoyed. In literature, both poetry and fiction moved steadily away from mere sequential telling of stories, into experiments with form which came to be grouped under the heading, 'stream of consciousness'. Woolf, Joyce, Eliot, Pound, Proust, Mallarme, Kafka and Rilke headed a conscious revolt against the traditions of the 19th century, and as a consequence became increasingly 'difficult' for the general public to appreciate and enjoy.

Post-modernism, or post-structuralism as Foucault would call it, has seemed a reaction in the fine arts against many of the tenets of modernism. It has seen a strong reaction against over-arching grand theories. Marx and Freud have lost some of their influence, although Fredric Jameson's 'Post-Modernism or The Cultural Logic of Late Capitalism' still clings to Marxist definitions. He regards modernism as the last flare of individualism in the arts, cheerfully regardless of whether the public appreciated the arts or not, and considers post-modern-ism as a sad descent into aesthetic populism, a merging of the fine arts and of 'pop' arts, which is depressingly bland. The OED defines post-modernism as 'a style and concept in the arts characterised by a distrust of theo-ries and ideologies, and by the drawing of attention to conventions'. New technology has arrived to help estab-lish new forms as well. Intermedia, installation art, conceptual art, multimedia, especially when involving video or DVD, all depend heavily on new technology, and reflect an encouraging attempt on the part of the fine arts to grapple with the new opportunities techno-logical change makes possible. There has also been a new willingness to return to traditional forms and styles, a willingness to 'pick and mix' in the form of 'bricollage', which particularly in architecture, has meant an often strange juxtaposition of different styles.

The Current Role of the Critic

I MMERSED AS THE modern art critic is in current waves of post-modernism, and having looked at the strange ways in which critics have affected the arts throughout Western cultural history, what is the present day art critic to make of his or her current role on the arts scene? The critic's existence as a practitioner on the aesthetic scene is now accepted, in ways that earlier centuries might not have found so philosophically respectable. From the 18th century onwards, Kant has made the 'aesthetic' sense something apart and different from our other range of responses. Roger Scruton, in his 'Judging Architecture', emphasises its difference. He points out that when we respond to wine, it is the taste of the wine to which we respond, and of course in the process we consume the wine. When we respond to a building, our experience of the building is something else. The building remains intact. We respond to it as something either aesthetically pleasing or not. The same applies to a painting. We pay attention to it as an object outside ourselves. Suppose we then read a perceptive account of the painting by a critic like Gombrich. It may well be that when we return to the painting itself, our response to it has changed. We see more in it than we did before. Our experience of the painting has changed. The aesthetic pleasure we get from responding to the painting is best understood as a particular mode of understanding. It is inextricably bound up with experience, preference and thought, and it would be difficult and unprofitable to try and distinguish one from the other. The point to notice here is that the full aesthetic experience can change, can in a sense be educated, and that critics like Gombrich can play an important part in that process. In this sense a good critic can clearly help in the appreciation of works of art.

Possible Territory

I T MIGHT ALSO be interesting, although verging on dangerous territory, for a modern critic to take a hard look at particular individuals who have come to dominate the art scene, and try and evaluate their influence and even ask whether overall they have had a good or a bad effect. John Steegman in 'Victorian Taste' has looked carefully at the influence of Sir Charles Eastlake. Almost nobody has even heard of him today, and yet in mid-Victorian times his influence on the art establishment of his day was widespread and decisive. Would it be profitable to attempt something similar today with a towering and all-pervasive figure like Pierre Boulez, to try and estimate this composer and conductor's wide-ranging effect on the development of modern music? Or in the realm of painting and sculpture, art galleries and the art market, to look at the significant rise of Nicholas Serota, and try to assess his influence for good or bad?

Differences within the Arts

THERE IS ALSO a natural division within the arts. Obviously artist have to live, and need money to support themselves. Most of us, unlike Ruskin, do not have rich fathers to support us. Yet some can manage more comfortably than others. Philip Larkin is not thought of as librarian, but as a poet, and yet he managed throughout his life to live on a librarian's salary and pension. Poetry was central to his life, but he did not depend on it for an income. In 2010 'The Guardian' selected and wrote about five up-and-coming playwrights. None of them were earning their living as playwrights, but were in fact earning money doing other jobs. There are other arts whose practitioners need to succeed and need to sell their products, in order to live. Plays, operas, ballets, films and television programmes come before a very effective judge and jury. If they do not put bums on seats, if they cannot attract a paying public, if they cannot achieve respectable ratings, then they fail, whatever the critics say. Not even the most well-intentioned Arts Council grant will continue, if performers face row upon row of empty seats. Composers and orchestras face much the same jury. If the audience fail to turn up, the whole enterprise founders. Yet composers, like authors, can continue writing, even in straitened circumstances like the young J.K Rowling writing away in cafés because home was too cold and uninviting. Critics for the performing arts know that the ultimate verdict lies not with them but with the paying public. They can hope to influence their readers, but ultimately in the performing arts, if the public does not like what is on offer, disaster will follow.

There are other arts where this is much less the case. The unappreciated painter slaving away in his garret, is a popular cliché, but it contains some truth.

There is also the whole questionable and sometimes positively corrupt world of art galleries and commercial art sales. The critic of painting and sculpture, already as we have seen, slightly demoralised by the abject failures of his predecessors, is uneasily part of the strange area of galleries and art sales, and yet hopefully able to stand outside them and try to take an objective view. Similarly literary critics, while inevitably part of the literary scene, can also persuade themselves they are trying hard to be objective. Authors need to find publishers, books need to sell to readers, but writers when reviewing their contemporaries, can at least try hard to be objective.

Accessibility

THERE IS ALSO the wider question of accessibility. In Britain we are small enough as an island to be able to ensure that the whole country is able to read the same paper at the same time, or jointly listen to the same radio programmes, or watch television together. This means that the media can offer a range of choices. There are a number of quality newspapers to pick from, different news channels, a choice of quality magazines, all equipped when necessary with their own arts critics. This means that any particular art work – a film, a book, a painting, a symphony, an opera, a ballet – will be reviewed by a number of different authoritative voices. In general they do not always agree. Some can be hostile, some can be supportive. This tends to have two results. Attentive readers or listeners in the media, coming across different viewpoints, are more inclined, after listening to the debate, to try and sample the art work for themselves and make up their own mind. Secondly they are also inclined to shop around within the arts media, until they find a critic who tends to be on their own wavelength, and with whom they feel in sympathy, and then they stick with that particular critic.

This is much healthier than the arts scene in New York, where one particular critic, because there is only one dominant quality newspaper, can with a hostile review in effect close down a theatre performance. It means that the relatively fewer critics in New York are treated with an exaggerated deference they do not really deserve, because they have an influence out of all proportion to their merit. I am actually sympathising with that ballerina who poured a bowl of punch over the head of Clive Barnes, then the dance and theatre critic of the 'New York Times'. If he was the only critic most theatre goers in New York read, his influence was by English standards, extraordinary. His influence came close to artistic tyranny, and the bowl of punch seems a very understandable response to that tyranny. It does seem surprising that a country which could produce the Boston Tea Party in response to what it saw as political tyranny, submits so meekly to something close to tyranny in its arts media. There is also a further irony in the fact that Barnes was not American at all, but English! Over here, when he was a critic for the 'Daily Express', he had much less influence on the English arts scene, at least partly because he was only one among a number of similar voices. It is a healthier situation, and it does mean that on the rare occasions when the critics all agree, the general public is more likely to take note.

There have too been occasions when the single voice of a single critic has made a surprising difference. Pinter's 'The Birthday Party' met with a chorus of disapproval when it first appeared, but a late review from Harold Hobson at the weekend managed to save it from oblivion and help it in the nick of time.

An Awareness of History

I HAVE EMPHASISED HOW important it is for arts critics to have a comprehensive background knowledge of the history of their art form. If anything could make them feel humble, it should be an awareness of history. Time and again, critics have had a disastrous influence on the development of their chosen art form. It was not just the Romantics who realised that an art form proceeds along a series of minor or major revolutions or rebellions. It has often taken time before different developments came to be fully appreciated. Attitudes and assumptions have had to change to catch up.

Critics set in their ways of thinking, too fully taken up with responding to the known and the already admired, have sometimes been all too ready to dismiss the new and the different simply because it is outside their experience. Yet ultimately a critic can only report on his own informed response. If he is genuinely unable to see what an artist is driving at, or cannot see any purpose that is worthwhile in the effort, then he must say so. Yet perhaps a knowledge of history will prevent him from saying it too loudly or too authoritatively. Ruskin could have told us he had no sympathy for what Whistler was trying to do, and did not feel it was worthwhile attempting to do it, but 'coxcomb', 'throwing a pot of paint in the public's face' was mud-slinging. It was also handing down judgement from a throne. It was precisely what critics should not be doing.

In architecture I find myself in sympathy with the Prince of Wales. In painting and sculpture I fully endorse the strictures of Robert Hughes, so brilliant in his analysis of so many of his contemporaries, but who is unable to enthuse over some of the more recent developments in these arts. Yet I cannot but be aware of the past, perched on my shoulder and gripping tightly to make sure I know it is there. The past can be mocking as well as seductive. 'Is the fault in you?' it asks, 'Like so many people in history, are you just unable to adjust to the new and the exciting? Are you too bogged down by what you think you know, to be able to adjust your mindset to change?' It is a nagging doubt the critic will take with him into the theatre, the cinema, the gallery, the concert hall, or when he opens a book or turns on the television. Yet in the last analysis, art is there to give us, as Longinus wrote so long ago, 'transports of delight'. We can all recognise them when they arrive like manna from heaven. It is the critic's job to report, celebrate and reflect on their arrival.